Another Facet – Painting in Water Colour

Contents

Contents

Picture Titles

Foreword

The name O S Nock is synonymous with railways. Mention his name to a group of railwaymen or railway enthusiasts in almost any country in the world and someone will have read one or more of his 140-odd books and most will be familiar with the name O S Nock the writer. But how many will be familiar with Ossie Nock the man? I suggest very few unless they have been fortunate enough to count him amongst their personal friends.

In this delightful book you will meet the man behind the well-known author, the warm sincere personality who not only loves railways but much else besides. The wild crags and rivers of Cumbria, the majesty of the Cornish coast. The peaceful beauty of his garden and the wild birds who feed there. A man whose interests range far beyond Claughtons, Compounds and Castles to include archaeology, astronomy, music and painting. Whose fluency with the pen is matched by his artistry with the brush. The real O S Nock, Ossie Nock, is superbly captured in the pages of this book and I am honoured to have been asked to contribute to it.

Ken Payne.

Preface

Looking back over the years it might seem that I was born with a pencil in my right hand. There is certainly no documentary evidence of my early attempts in draughtmanship until about the year 1912, when I was seven years old. Then a present of *The Wonder Book of Ships* evidently fired me with such enthusiasm for big Transatlantic liners that I copied some of the fine colour plates in that book, and coloured my drawings with crayons. I do not know what subsequently happened to those coloured drawings until, some forty years later when my father died, we were left with a mass of paperwork of all kinds and interests and those old coloured drawings of ships were in the heap. They were still in remarkably good condition and so I inserted them near the flyleaf of a large book and forgot all about them. Fortunately I remembered where I had put them, but there they remained for another 37 years and then I extracted them in the present context.

I had already drafted a number of pieces on some of my favourite paintings when the post brought the autumn edition of *Wildlife Matters*, the magazine of the David Shepherd Conservation Foundation for endangered mammals. My dear Nerrida, the loving companion of my old age, was keenly interested, and as she is a connoisseur of books herself I got out from my library his two books *The Man who loves Giants* and *A Brush with Steam*, the last mentioned which he kindly autographed and included a touching condolence to my own then recent bereavement. Then I pulled out for Nerrida his great book *David Shepherd, the Man and His Paintings*. Turning over the pages of that sumptuous volume once again I thought: 'Who am I, the merest amateur artist, to think of writing a book about *my* paintings!' It is true that several of my purely railway subjects have been reproduced in various of my own semi-technical books, but a whole book about them, no, definitely no! Then I came to recall that Nerrida's cousin, a very old family friend, an engineer, and a highly skilled builder and operator of model railways, had read some of the drafts of my preliminary chapters. He has in his own library some of my own books, and he said several times that my projected 'Painting in Water Colours' would be his favourite of them all, because it somehow revealed me, as the personality behind the technical writing in other books. So, I determined to go ahead.

So going back to my boyhood, documentary evidence of my further progress in draughtmanship had not been preserved in the family archives until my parents had moved from Reading to Barrow-in-Furness and I was a boarder at Giggleswick School. Then each year when I came home for the Christmas holidays one of my first self-imposed tasked was to draw, and latterly to paint a calendar to hang behind my mother's small private desk in the dining room. In the later years of my time at Giggleswick they had one of those beautiful 'Windsor and Newton' type sketching boards ready for me to work upon. The calendars for the years 1921 and 1922 have fortunately been kept, and are reproduced herewith. The last mentioned was done after I had left Giggleswick and was a first-year engineering student at Imperial College in South Kensington. Looking at the pictures I painted then, at the present time, I have no idea what the subjects are, or from where I got the ideas. The 1921 card looks as if it might be somewhere in the Alps except that the tall bushy elm trees have a distinctly English flavour. The 1922 picture is characteristic of the bleak, snowy moonlit scenes very frequently favoured by Christmas-card artists at the time. At my present age the picture makes me hope that the inmates of that picturesque cottage had got some efficient central heating in their rooms!

So that is how it all started. Before then I had tried my hand at painting trains in motion, in colour, copying photographs published in *The Railway Magazine* and adding my own colour. But I am not very proud of some of the results I produced, prior to 1921. One of the best at that early stage was one of the Caledonian 'Cardean' class

Calendar 1921: Scene somewhere in the Alps.

CALENDAR. 1922.

Calendar 1922: Winter night scene.

4-6-0 on the 10 a.m. Glasgow to Euston express near Symington. Unfortunately I had never seen a Caledonian engine 'in the flesh' as it were, and painted my picture in the dark blue livery shown in various colour books and picture postcards.

My parents were not all that keen on my painting trains and locomotives, and I began to copy pictures from some of my father's books. I remember he gave me *The Nature Book*, a lovely production, published by Cassell and Co in 1908! In it was a beautiful colour-plate of a pool in the New Forest which I was keen to copy. It was an ambitious project for a relative beginner like me, but my father was pleased with the result, and had it framed. Where it went I have no idea now. I fancy it must have been given away in one of our house removals. Then I began to paint some of the scenes I photographed on our various summer holidays, and these are reproduced in this book.

At first I thought to include only the non-railway subjects, seeing that some of the railway ones now hanging on my walls on my present home have already been reproduced in my books. But my friends who are encouraging me to go on were insistent that some of these, at any rate, should be included. So to Ken Payne, his cousin, my dear Nerrida, to Eric Harris and Jim Waller and all others of who have wished me well in this my 143rd book, greetings and many thanks.

O S Nock

Chapter 1
Newby Bridge

It could not have been more than a month after the family house removal from Reading to Barrow-in-Furness when on a Saturday at lunch my father announced that he was proposing to make a trip to Windermere that same afternoon. Of course my young sister and I were excited at the very idea, but my mother who at the time had posed an attitude of indifference, sometimes I regret to add amount to outright rudeness, to any local Furnessian associations or topography, stayed at home. The three of us walked down to Furness Abbey Station, caught a local train, and changed to the Lakeside Branch train at Ulverston. My father had always been an inveterate collector, and once installed in Barrow he began amassing brochures, and picture postcards, and in this respect the Furness Railway was second to none among the pre-grouping lines of Great Britain in publicizing the scenic attractions of the districts it served. As a mere junior schoolboy I became conscious of the way in which my father had read-up the topography of the line from Ulverston to Lakeside, and when we were leaving the station at Haverthwaite, where the present preserved line to Lakeside begins, he said that there was a very pretty bridge to be seen beside the next station, Newby Bridge.

Actually the station there was a single platform without any cross-over or points and no signals. We could not see much of the bridge or the river during the brief time when the train was at the platform, and in any case my sister and I were then agog to get on to Lakeside and the steamer in which we were to sail up to Ambleside. Before leaving Reading I had learned to ride a push-bicycle, but at first,

during the school holidays, I did not go far from our new home near
Furness Abbey. It was when my father gave me a folding Brownie
camera that took postcard-size photographs that I began to venture
farther afield. The distance from our home to Newby Bridge was 17
miles, and I found I could do the distance, out and home, comfort-
ably between meal times, between breakfast and midday lunch, or
between lunch and 'nursery tea', which was plenty of time to pause
on the way to take photographs of the many attractive scenes between Greenodd and Newby Bridge, which latter place I had found
was seen very far from its best from the railway.

By that time my father had purchased a copy of the magnificent
colour-book published by A & C Black on 'The English Lakes'. The
artist, A Heaton Cooper, lived in the district and there were two
beautiful pictures of his at Newby Bridge. One of them showed the
bridge itself, and in the background the Swan Hotel, but the second,
a particularly charming picture, was evidently painted from one of
the upper rooms in the hotel looking across the bridge. Black's
made this exquisite painting the frontispiece in their beautiful book.
One fine spring day, when I was in the Easter vacation from Imperial
College in London, I rode out towards Newby Bridge to take photographs of some well remembered scenes. From Ulverston my road
took me towards the wide sandy estuary of the River Kent which
brings the waters of Windermere to Morecambe Bay. My first stopping place was usually the little village of Greenodd, where the River
Crake, bringing down the waters of Coniston lake debouches into
the Kent estuary. It was a very pretty place providing many scenes for
attractive photographs. At Greenodd the main road, and also the
branch line of the Furness Railway, took a right-angle turn eastwards
to cross a stretch of level country before entering the rocky and very
picturesque valley that leads up to the foot of Windermere. I had
been this way by train several times previously, but the road sparsely
used as it always was then, gave plenty of time for sightseeing.

On a later occasion, when unfortunately I had not got my camera
with me, I was passing Greenodd station when the signals were
pulled off for a train bound for Lakeside Windermere. From my
knowledge of the usual timetable for the branch I realized that this
was not one of the regular passenger trains so I rode on over the

bridge crossing the River Crake and stopped where I had a broadside view of the line where it crossed a low viaduct on the entrance to the estuary itself. I did not have long to wait. From my viewpoint on the road I had an almost head-on view of the line approaching Greenodd station, which was double tracked from the Plumpton triangle junction with the main line. I saw that the approaching passenger train was much longer than anything I had seen on the branch previously. It was not stopping at Greenodd, but slowing down to collect the token for the single line section that began at that station. It was entirely a Midland train, headed by a rebuilt 4-4-0 locomotive hauling a train of those beautiful clerestory-roofed carriages. I cannot remember how many there were of them, but as usual they were very clean and made a picture. There were three men on the footplate. I imagined they were the regular Midland men, accompanied by a road-pilotman who had joined them at Carnforth. I was sorry I had no time to ride on to Lakeside on that day, and see the train in more leisurely conditions.

Riding on from Greenodd, on the former occasion I entered the narrow valley of the River Kent at Haverthwaite. There was a picturesque church to be photographed there, though many times lately when I have been reading of the developments with the Lakeside and Haverthwaite preserved railway have I recalled my father's oft repeated 'crack' when we were travelling to and from Lakeside in my boyhood years, and the trains we used were frequently held up because of another train which was crossing on the single line section, and with which we had got to exchange tokens, was running late. 'Haverthwaite,' always exclaimed my father, 'where we have a wait!' There was not much else to photograph in the village in my cycling days, but further east there was the remarkable industrial complex of Backbarrow, the principal reason, I believe, why the branch was constructed at all. It was one of the first new enterprises undertaken when the original Furness Railway had taken over the Whitehaven and Furness Junction and the Ulverston and Lancaster, in 1860. First of all, a few miles beyond Haverthwaite, were the iron works so secretly hidden between the railway and the river than on my first bicycle rides in this district I was unaware of their existence. If I then had referred to my father's one-inch Ordnance Survey map of the district I would have seen their location clearly marked, in fact their origin, I was told, went back to the year 1711!

Small iron working plants, I learned, were located in many seemingly unlikely places in the Furness and West Cumberland districts, and the fuel they used was charcoal. In the second of Black's magnificent colour-books about the district, *Wild Lakeland*, published in 1922, there is a whole chapter dealing with charcoal-burning from certain selected forest trees, and a beautiful reproduction of one of Heaton Cooper's delightful paintings showing the process used in the woodlands. The charcoal thus produced was bagged up and sent from the remote sites to the iron works needing it. I am told that before construction of the branch line railways much of the charcoal used for firing the blast furnace at Backbarrow was processed in tree plantations near Coniston, brought down by water to the foot of the lake, and taken by road to the iron works. I understand that the plant at Backbarrow had been closed down in the early 1900s, but was re-opened in the emergency of the First World War. Subsequently, until its final closure in the 1960s, the fuel used was coke rather than charcoal.

Just beyond the site of the iron works the road made a sharp S-bend to cross the river. It would in any case be a place for cautious running because of the narrowness of the road, but on both sides of the road there were buildings of the Backbarrow washing-blue works. Not only did the walls obscure the way ahead across and beyond the S-curve of the bridge itself but they had been built right out to the roadway providing no space for a footpath on either side. From hindsight, viewed many years after my push-bicycling days, it would seem a death trap! In my younger days the 'blue-works' was very aptly named. The dust from it stained everything: the walls, the windows, the men and women who worked there, the road extending far beyond that villainous S-curve, the hedges, the water in the river, and even the ducks which were bred locally. To avoid getting myself coated I used to approach that potentially lethal S-curve at the highest speed I could manage, about 20 m.p.h., and in knowledge of the virtual absence of any other traffic tear between the buildings and round the S-curve sounding my bell for all it was worth!

Having passed this brief hazard the remaining hilly miles on to Newby Bridge, with the river near at hand, were delightful, and my camera was in active use at once. I took pictures of the bridge itself from many angles and then crossed to the farther side of the river. I could not of course emulate Heaton Cooper's viewpoint and get a glimpse of the very pretty bridge from an upper-floor window, but from the forecourt of the hotel I was able to get an attractive view across the river with a lovely bank of wild daffodils on the shore in the immediate foreground. I recalled from my school poetry days that Wordsworth had written a piece about daffodils, and after I had returned home and the films had been developed in the jury-rigged darkroom in the bathroom of my parent's home, I looked out one of my school treasures, *The Oxford Book of English Verse,* and enjoyed once again Wordsworth's charming poem, entitled just *Daffodils.*

It was not until very many years later that I, personally, learned the origin of that little masterpiece. In 1947 Olivia and I, having parked both children upon some very friendly neighbours, escaped from the rigours of post-war industrial matters for a single week in the Lake District. Browsing round a shop in Ambleside I came across a newly published book about the Lakes. It was described as an anthology of lakeland life and landscape. It was illustrated throughout in colour, and as the paintings were attractive and beautifully reproduced I bought it, for this reason alone. Then I found that this anthology contained much reading matter that was of interest, particularly a piece entitled *Dancing Daffodils,* by Dorothy Wordsworth, sister of the ever-memorable poet. In it she describes how her brother's celebrated piece came to be written, as a result of a walk one wild threatening day, not anywhere near Newby Bridge but on the banks of Ullswater near Gowbarrow Park. I am glad that the daffodils came clearly out in my photograph though on this particular day, calm in early spring, they were not dancing at all.

The proposal that the branch line of the railway should terminate at Newby Bridge was short lived, and before construction had proceeded so far authority had been obtained for a continuation to the side of the lake, and for erection of a jetty at which small vessels could berth. I enjoyed many trips on the steam yachts owned and operated by the Furness Railway, but at least one author, who lived for a time in the Lake District and who should have known better, seemingly became confused over this. Doreen Wallace at the end of the 1930s contributed a racy and beautifully illustrated book *English Lakeland* in Batsford's *Face of Britain* series. In it she wandered as far off the actual Lakeland track as Furness Abbey, and incidentally made some remarks about Barrow which drew the wrath of the civic authorities there to such an extent that a public apology and a reprint of the book were demanded! I myself would have hesitated to join issue with such a forthright controversialist as Doreen Wallace had she been still alive, but in her book she tells of boarding the steamer for Ambleside at *Newby Bridge*, and how she found the south end of Windermere was 'pretty rather than grand, but so pretty'. Scenery apart however not even the smallest of the Furness Railway steam yachts, even the little *Gondola* which sailed on Coniston Lake, could have got as far down the River Leven as Newby Bridge.

Once firmly established in Barrow my father began to build up his collection of books about the Lake District, and one of those which I was allowed to read was one of the *Highways and Byways* series published by the Macmillans in 1901, on the Lake District written by A G Bradley. Despite an otherwise delightful book, in which the author's only motive power was a push-bicycle, he was precluded by accident, not in the course of the trip (!), from concluding his survey in the Furness district, although he had previously made a not very enjoyable passage through Newby Bridge. Then after cycling from the lovely village of Hawkshead to the Western shores of Windermere he can tell the tale of his misfortunes, thus: 'At the Ferry a road turns to the right, and the actively disposed with time upon their hands might well be tempted to follow it to the foot of Windermere, and so back upon the further bank to Bowness, whither we are now bound, and can, moreover, reach in ten minutes if we so choose. But I would urge them rather to explore the beauties of the lake's lower end by water. For though it may seem strange that no highway follows the course of this half of the most famous and most frequented sheet of water in England, this is practically the case, for the road, which starts from the Ferry in such promising fashion, carries you through an almost continuous screen of woods, and by steep gradients that for this reason you climb to no purpose. I speak feelingly, having

Newby Bridge, an early spring scene from the hotel forecourt.

once made this mistake and, though the details of this secluded road have escaped my memory, being in truth somewhat monotonous, the regrettable state of mental heat in which I found myself at Newby Bridge has not. The road back to Bowness upon the other side looks beautiful upon the map; but the lie of the country and the earlier struggles of this same highway to grapple with it which are very conspicuous from across the lake, would certainly confirm them in recommending anyone to see the beauties of Lower Windermere by boat.

Before I came to read this part of the book I had some experience of one of the roads in question, and unfortunately on that occasion I was not the only participant. Before she was married my mother was an ardent and expert cyclist and she hoped my sister and I would follow suit. My sister always averred that what big brother can do I can do even better, so when a joint trip to Lakeside was planned my mother gave her full approval. It was not, of course, to be one of my out-and-home between meals exercises but a more leisurely trip taking a picnic lunch with us. At this distance in time I cannot remember if we had previously planned to continue our explorations beyond Lakeside, but when we arrived at the pier one of the steam yachts was almost ready to depart, so we humped our bicycles on board, and on a pleasant spring day enjoyed the sail up the lake as far as Bowness. The ride back to Newby Bridge would have prolonged our homeward journey by no more than about 7 miles and we set off with high hearts, but what a road! Bradley in his *Highways and Byways* did not exaggerate the difficulties. It was horrible, I should think, that in those 7 miles to Newby Bridge we spent at least 2 pushing our bicycles by hand up those fearsome gradients. Both of us were hot and exhausted by the time we got to Newby Bridge.

In the previous school term, my last winter at Giggleswick, I had been awarded my house colours in Rugby Football and continuing to feel very fit I was game for any amount of physical exertion on holiday. Just after the trip to Bowness, the weather continuing fine, I decided to ride over to the London and North Western main line to try my hand at photographing some of the trains there. A study of my Ordnance Survey map showed me there was a direct, if somewhat hilly road branching off from the main highway little more than a mile from Newby Bridge, which reduced the distance to Kendal to about 10 miles, compared to almost double the distance when using the main road over Lindale to near Grange-over-Sands and then across the marshes to Levens Bridge and the road up from Lancaster. But I wonder what A G Bradley would have thought of the road over the fells that I took to Kendal that day? From where it branched off, then at river level, it climbed about 650 feet in about 1 mile to reach the summit near the crag of Gummers How. For me it was an accent on the 'push' all the way up here, but having arrived, although my principal project that day was railway photography, I had to spare at least one exposure for the magnificent prospect from the summit there looking over the foot of Windermere and the windings of the River Leven down to Newby Bridge.

After graduation, and obtaining employment in Central London, I continued to live at the same Toc H Mark in South Kensington where I had been during the four years of my student days, but there was a big difference. Gone for ever were the days when I could pack my bag and go up to Barrow for three or four weeks at Christmas and Easter and for a break at least three times as long in the summer vacation. In the London office of Westinghouse all staff from the highest to the most lowly paid got two weeks holiday, except for those hoary old stagers classed as Veterans, and they got a total of three weeks. Having been in Toc H for more than four years and been accordingly accepted with some degree of seniority. I had been allocated to a little private bed-sit on the top floor of the five-storey mansion that was rented in Queens Gate Gardens. It was a pleasant little den, for the seclusion it gave at times. From the outset of my association with Toc H I had embarked thoroughly in the activities of social service, sport, and regular meetings that were involved, not in any sense of obligation but rather as the 'way of life' that had to come to me at that time. Even so I was glad of the bed-sit, at odd moments. My first months as a Graduate Trainee at Westinghouse were far from happy, and I welcomed a place where I could occasionally have a private 'think'.

I had taken some of my photography albums with me, and also my box of water colours with its accompanying palettes, and occasionally on Sunday morning I did some painting. My first essay in this direction was to sketch the view from the hotel forecourt at Newby Bridge with the daffodils on the river bank much in evidence. I pencilled in the outline of the scene, and then came a break. The Westinghouse London Office was always closed on the Tuesdays after a Bank Holiday, and on those occasions I braved crowded trains and late running to pay a visit to Barrow. While I was at home on this particular visit I sought out my father's book *Highways and Byways in the Lake District* and turning to the artist's drawing of Newby Bridge saw to my surprise a very large and bushy elm tree on the downstream side of the river. There was certainly no trace of it, even of the stump in my photograph. I sometimes wondered if it had been put there by artist's license. I took my own water-colour home on my next visit, and when going home for Christmas that same year I was honoured to see it framed and hanging on one of the walls.

Chapter 2

Dartmouth – The Butterwalk

July 1925 was my last holiday before I went to work with Westinghouse. I was due to report for duty at the head office near Kings Cross Station in the last week before the August Bank Holiday weekend while my sister, then at school at Sutton, Surrey, finished her summer term at almost exactly the same time. My parents decided on Paignton for my father's month that year, and it was arranged that I should spend the first fortnight with them and that my sister would arrive, unfortunately, the same weekend that I was departing for London. In those pre-war years Westinghouse always extended the break after a bank holiday to the Wednesday morning. So after my first week of duty in my new job I went off to Paignton for another long weekend.

The first fortnight was one of glorious weather. It would be an exaggeration to say I was hardly ever off the saddle of my bicycle, because I obviously had time to browse in a fine bookshop in one of Paignton's main streets, and to buy a magnificent book on the Moorlands, Streams and Coasts of Devon by Lady Rosalind Northcote. It was sumptuously illustrated in colour by a local artist, Frederick J Widgery, but I was made conscious of its limitations by a paragraph on the very first page of the book, in which the author wrote: 'My position is that of a person who had been bidden to take from a great heap of precious stones as many as are needed to make one chain; for however grasping that person may be, and however long the chain may be made, when all the stones have been chosen, the heap will look almost as great and delightful as before: only a few of the largest and brightest jewels will be gone.'

10

Every years before setting out for the chosen district for that year's monthly holiday, my father always bought one of the voluminous pocket guide books then published by Ward, Locke and Co at one shilling each, if I remember it rightly! They were literally packed with information maps, town and district plans and hundreds of photographs. Even before the time came for us to leave home for our holiday haunt I had devoured the guide books about the Torquay district, and planned in advance the places to which I was going to ride in the next fortnight. The only trouble was that sessions of railway photography had also to be included. The Great Western Railway had given me walking passes over certain picturesque stretches of line including the fascinating coastal length between Dawlish and Teignmouth, including the tunnels, of which I have a particular story to tell! But we had barely arrived in Paignton by 'The Torbay Limited', as it was then known, around 4 p.m. on a Friday afternoon before I was riding off in a first reconnaissance.

But before leaving Paignton station, on our first arrival, I was intrigued to see the big express engine, which had done us proud on the fast and exacting run down from Paddington non-stop to Exeter, coupling off to be replaced by a dumpy little 2-6-2 tank engine, the very antithesis of what a handsome Great Western locomotive should look like. I had previously seen these little engines working on branch trains in Cornwall, but here was one of them coupling on to the seven palatial 70-foot bogie corridor coaches of 'The Torbay Limited' and heading out into the blue, south of Paignton. I learned afterwards that there were then no facilities for turning the large express engines at the end of this branch line.

My first expedition was no more than a short one, over the hills next to Torbay, past the branch line junction of Churston and on to where I got a first sight of the estuary of the River Dart. Fascinated by the scene I free-wheeled down the steep hill into Kingswear. I have many times subsequently echoed the sentiments I afterwards read in Lady Northcote's books: 'Although upon all parts of the South Hams there hovers a spell that is inexplicable, perhaps it is felt more in Dartmouth than in any other place one can think of. Possibly it is the loveliness of sea and land, flowers in the crevices of the cliffs hanging low towards the water's edge, the grey tower rising out of the sea, the

picturesqueness of the town, with its thronging associations, or just
the intangible influences of bygone days.' I did not cross on the ferry
that evening but I saw enough of that delightful waterfront to entice
me to go across, soon, armed with plenty of rolls of film. But that
same evening I looked out across the spacious main anchorage over
by the palatial buildings of the Royal Naval College, and I did not
then think how relatively soon it would be before that historic anchorage would be chosen as one of the bases from which one of the
biggest amphibious combined Naval and Military operation has ever
set forth from these islands, in 1944.

Inevitably, I suppose, my attention was drawn to the small terminal
station of the branch line railway on the waterfront at Kingswear. At
a first glance it appeared nondescript, but some days later, exercis-
ing my walking permit, I found some intriguing details of when the
line was a branch of the South Devon Railway. This line which was
absorbed by the Great Western in 1878 had its engineering and
administrative headquarters at Newton, but although the final
change-over from the broad gauge, originally conceived by Brunel,
had taken place more than thirty years previously there were still
some sidings laid with the old 'Bridge' rails designed by Brunel, and
many odd lengths of that type of rail used as fencing posts and such.
I photographed the arrival of 'The Torbay Limited' at Kingswear,
and some little time afterward the same 2-6-2 tank engine leaving
bunker first on the local train to Newton Abbot, which carried the
two through carriages which provided the last evening service from
the Torbay line to Paddington. However it is high time we were done
with trains, and crossing the river to the Dartmouth waterfront.

Once off the ferry before beginning to explore the lovely old town
I had to take a new look at the river itself, of the picturesque grouping of the relatively new, but beautifully placed, houses of Kingswear
up the hillside and the exquisite sweep of the river itself down to its
mouth with the guardian castles of Kingswear and Dartmouth standing almost theatrically pretty on each steep hillside. There were
subjects galore for my camera there, but now I turned my attention
to the town. First, there was the utterly fascinating Butter Walk. One
was attracted at once by the way the upper stories of the buildings jut
out quite across the pavements and rest upon columns, making

The Butterwalk, Dartmouth, some fifteen years before the serious damage caused by a German bomb.

piazzas or covered ways along the street. Such a form of construction is rare in England, but I later found another example of it not very far away, in Totnes, further upstream on the River Dart. My photographic apparatus then did not permit of a picture inside the piazza, but I secured a nice shot looking westwards along the scene, which I afterwards committed to a water-colour painting.

At the time when I did this picture, the late autumn of 1925, I was evidently more concerned about what could be termed photographic accuracy rather than a work of art, as such. Otherwise I should never have included the garish garage sign that intrudes from the corner of the house nearest to the waterfront. All I did was to soften the rude colours in the placard. It was not until after World War II when I purchased the fine Batsford book on Dartmouth written by Percy Russell that I read the history of the building of the Butter Walk. But that book was not published until 1950, and before, then staying with my young family in a hotel on the seafront at Teignmouth, we had visited Dartmouth, by train to Kingswear this time, and I had been appalled by the damage caused to the magnificent façade of the main frontage of the Butter Walk, apparently by a quite isolated German bomb. It was all shuttered up and looking horrible. My dear Olivia, familiar enough with the painting that hung on one of the walls at home, was horrified!

A visit to Dartmouth that we both made in 1957 was very much of a railway occasion, for me especially. The historic, record-breaking G.W.R. locomotive *City of Truro* had been extracted from the Railway Museum at York, and at Swindon Works put into full working order again; so much so that when she was earmarked for a Sunday excursion from Swindon to Kingswear and back, the locomotive inspector in charge of the trip was hoping for a record speed in descending the Wellington Bank on the return journey. I had a footplate pass to ride the engine between Bristol and Kingswear in both directions while Olivia rode in the train behind. Once arrived at the well-loved estuary, as soon as I had a wash (!) we took the ferry and enjoyed the pleasance of a beautiful day in early summer on that well-remembered waterfront, from which I was glad to see that the wartime damage to the Butter Walk had been repaired. Incidentally, we did 84 m.p.h. down the Wellington Bank on the way home. This was some considerable way short of the 102 m.p.h. reached in 1904, but on that Sunday we had a load more than twice as heavy as that of the *Ocean Mail* of more than 50 years earlier.

My last visit to Dartmouth and my last contemplation of the architectural beauties of the Butter Walk came in a motoring tour some years later, which began believe it or not, at Derby! I had been riding on some of the new diesel locomotives working over the beautiful route through the Peak District to Manchester. Olivia was with me, not on the footplate I hasten to add, not at any rate on a diesel (!), and our first holiday stop was at Stratford-on-Avon to enjoy a play at the Shakespeare Memorial Theatre. There we were joined by our great friend of wartime Chippenham days, Eve Arrowsmith. Next day we drove down to Beaulieu in the New Forest, when the increasing sultriness in the air, presaging an oncoming storm, did nothing to mar our enjoyment of the beautiful woodlands we were passing through. The thunder came in the night and, as frequently happens, the morning all was wonderfully fresh and clear afterwards. We drove to Dartmouth that day and arriving about teatime booked in at the Royal Castle Hotel on the waterfront and within easy walking distance for another look at the Butter Walk. On the following morning before we left for the Far West there was time to take Eve down the lane leading to St Petrock's Church and the castle. Looking out over the estuary to where Kingswear Castle used to guard the opposite bank of the river, and drinking in the sheer beauty of the scene we wondered if there was a lovelier place in all England than that we were then beholding!

Now back to Torbay, and I do not think I can do better in opening than to quote again from Lady Northcote's book: 'It is impossible for those who have had no better fortune than to see Torbay only in prints on photographs to gather more than a very imperfect idea of what its best can be. The cliffs near Paignton are red, nearer Torquay they are a warm russet, alternating with a rosy grey where limestone comes to the surface; and some of the rocks beneath, shining with salt water, are pink interlined with white veins. In fair weather the warm tints of these cliffs, chequered by a green lattice-work of plants and bushes, and the rich full colours of the sea make a picture that is more easily remembered than described.'

Chapter 3
Midland Scotch Express Nearing Ais Gill Summit

For all my childish love of geography in my early years I had not a clue as to where Ais Ghyll was, or as I came to know it later on the nameboards of the signal box, Ais Gill. Then in the late summer, when I was with my parents on holiday at Weymouth, there came news of the collision between two southbound Midland Scotch expresses in the middle of the night near Ais Gill. I was far too young then to appreciate what had happened, but I have a vivid recollection of the graphic way the artist correspondent of our own paper, I believe it was *The Daily Mail*, portrayed the scene with the engine of the second train standing like some evil genius amid the blazing carriages into which it had collided, and in which many passengers were burnt to death before they could be rescued. The newspapers piled on the agony, to the embarrassment of the top management of the Midland Railway, by recalling that only some three years earlier, not more than three or four miles to the south of Ais Gill in the early hours of Christmas Eve, 1910, another collision had taken place when damage to the gas-lighted carriages of the Midnight Scotch Express from London to Glasgow caused another fire, and the deaths of many passengers who were trapped in the wreckage. For me Ais Gill made a greater impression on my boyish sentiments than the sinking of the *Titanic* which took place in the same summer.

Three years after Ais Gill I was enrolled as a boarder at Giggleswick School, within sight of the now-famed Settle and Carlisle railway, the line that climbs to its summit on Ais Ghyll moor, 1100 ft. above sea

15

level on the borders of Yorkshire and Westmoreland, some 25 miles north of Settle itself. In term time the railway stations of Settle and Giggleswick (on the cross-country line to Carnforth and the Lake District) were out of bounds, so that any 'train-spotting' had to be done from a distance. But in the library in the junior house in which I was at first placed was a bequest collection that contained many railway books, and in my off-duty hours I learned much of locomotive history and particularly of the Midland Railway the engines of which could occasionally be seen from afar on some of our walks or field expeditions. At home my parents bought The *Railway Magazine* each month to further my education in this respect when I came home for the school holidays.

In due course in reading this then fabulous source of information I found that sometimes notices appeared about the availability of 'back numbers' of the magazine and as if my collection of current issues were not sufficiently cluttering up the shelves in my bedroom at home I spent some of my pocket money on selected 'back numbers'. Then when I went to Imperial College in London, in 1921, I found that one of my college libraries had many bound volumes of *The Railway Magazine* extending back far earlier than my own readership, and as lunch those days usually consisted of little more than a snack often the rest of the lunch hour was spent browsing through early volumes of this publication. In 1913 I found in the 'British Locomotive Practice and Performance' features a long account of running on the Midland Railway between Leeds and Carlisle. This was before news came through of the collision and fire at Ais Gill but still more important to me was a photograph of a southbound Scotch express approaching Ais Gill summit, the very place where the accident occurred. Until then I had never seen what this very bleak part of the line looked like.

The photographer in this case was R J Purves who, I later knew, was a signal engineer on the staff of the North Eastern Railway, and later of the North Eastern Area of the London and North Eastern Railway. Before the First World War I found reproductions of many of his superb photographs of North Eastern locomotives and trains, but in those early years evidently his funds precluded his going further afield than his own railway, on which passes were available, and his excursions to other areas were around Carlisle, and a single visit to the High Pennine reaches of the Midland Railway which could be reached by way of the branch line of the NER leading to Hawes Junction. From there he had to walk on the cross-country road to reach the Midland line north of Ais Gill. Later, from Westinghouse business I came to know him well, when he was Assistant Signal Engineer, and he gave me prints of many of his pre-war photographs, including the one of the up Midland Scotch express that had so taken my fancy in my student days. He was so intrigued that I had painted the scene in water colours that before going to York on one of my business visits I took the picture out of its frame and put it with the other papers I was taking in my briefcase.

The train he photographed, and I painted, was the 11 a.m. departure from Glasgow St Enoch, and over the Midland line it had a combination of engines that I have never seen personally nor depicted in photographs within my own ken. It was not so much the engines themselves as the way they were marshalled. The leading one was a 6ft. 6in. Deeley rebuild of one of Johnson's supremely beautiful '2203' class of 1893, a sister engine of that 446 that caused so much havoc at Ais Gill in 1913. My picture included No. 442. They had a very heavy train and on the Midland at that time it had to be double-headed. The almost invariable way was to put the assistant engine in the lead, but on this virtually unique occasion the helper, one of the Johnson 6ft. 8in. 2-4-0s of the '1400' class, was marshalled next to the train. I have often wondered what happened when they reached Ais Gill signal box and did not think to ask Purves if he remembered. Normally Midland trains coming from Carlisle stopped to detach their leading engines, where there was then plenty of siding accommodation; but on the day of Purves's photograph if the 4-4-0 No. 442 had actually coupled off the 2-4-0 would have been left with a somewhat staggering load, even though most of the run onwards to Hellifield is steeply downhill.

I should imagine that the original photograph was taken at a busy weekend in the summer because the regular rake of joint 'M & G & SW' corridor coaches had been 'strengthened', to use the term used in railway parlance for the addition of extra stock to a prescribed coach formation, by the addition of three flat-roofed bogies ahead of the usual corridor stock with their characteristic clerestory roofs, variously of Clayton and Bain design. I imagine that if F Moore, or any other railway artists of that period, had painted a picture of that train he would have ignored those leading coaches and rendered the whole train in the standard Midland style; but as shown in the colour reproduction I painted those leading coaches as Purves photographed them. I must confess that I have never been able to pinpoint their origin with any certainty. I think they must have been of Glasgow and South Western stock, added at the last minute to the train when the rush of passengers at St Enoch station overflowed the regular formation.

I had never been near Ais Gill in my time at Giggleswick, nor did I see in *The Railway Magazine* or anywhere else for that matter, any more photographs in the locality. From the Ordnance Survey Map in my growing collection I learned that the lofty ridge in the background of my painting went by the resounding name of Wild Boar Fell, and its summit was 2324 ft. above sea level, thus more than 1000 ft. above the railway at this point. On one of the motoring trips we made with our next door neighbours in Barrow when I was home for a Bank Holiday weekend we went first through Kendal, then near to the track of the West Coast main line above the Lune Valley and the much-photographed stretch of line including the water-troughs south of Tebay, then eastwards still following the Lune to its Watershed between it and the tributaries of the Carlisle Eden near Ravenstone Dale. Then on to the crossing of the Midland main line at Kirkby Stephen station, a station however a good two miles south of the pleasant little market town of that name. When crossing the railway, only some 8 miles north of Ais Gill summit, I looked southwards up the Eden Valley but nearby fells blocked the view towards the head of the dale.

My first through journey from Leeds to Carlisle was made on the night express from St Pancras to Edinburgh, and while all the intermediate stations were then fully manned they were then in darkness, and I could also not see any of the scenery. Nor was it much better when I came back a fortnight later. This time I travelled by the 12 noon from Edinburgh Waverley, and although I had a window corner it was on the wrong side of the train to see the mileposts from

In the High Pennines: a pre-grouping double-headed Midland express nearing Ais Gill summit 1151 ft. above sea-level.

Carlisle southwards. It was on a Saturday and the train was very crowded, and there was no chance of nipping across the carriage to spot the occasional milepost. My notes as to the speed were having to be made by counting the rail joints, and as our two engines were making a notable climb with what was then a heavy combined load from both Edinburgh and Glasgow I was kept very busy with no more than casual glances at the passing scenery. As we neared the summit of the line I was no more than vaguely aware that we were passing beneath the crags of Wild Boar Fell, then we were stopping at Ais Gill box to detach our pilot engine. From then onwards, until the onset of World War II, I was often travelling over the line, once in the guard's brake van of a night express goods, non-stop from Hellifield to Kingmoor Yard, north of Carlisle. I got to know the magnificent profiles of the mountain ranges we passed, but still there were no photographs, even when the new LMS 4-6-0 types began to supersede the old Midland 4-4-0s, and some of the newer compounds as well.

This in retrospect could have been regarded as surprising, seeing that the route received frequent and comprehensive reference in the 'British Locomotive Practice and Performance' feature in *The Railway Magazine* in the mid-1920s when the LMS were running trials with several non-Midland classes of express locomotives, ostentatiously to prove that the 3-cylinder compound of Derby design was the finest and most efficient type then owned by the LMS. At one time, indeed, the Operating Department, the personnel of which after the amalgamations of 1923 had a strongly Midland bias, was even considering reorganizing the entire train service, with moderate loads, that could be handled by the new standard compound 4-4-0s. The fact that the Leeds-Carlisle interchange running was not photographed could be accounted for mainly because the trials were not in any way publicized, that they took place in mid-winter and that the return journeys were made after dark.

It was not until George Lake began his somewhat venturesome publication of the new magazine *Railways*, in the late autumn of 1939 of all dates(!), that photographs taken on the mountain section of the Settle and Carlisle line began to appear in print. These were from Maurice Earley, to illustrate my first articles in the eventually long running 'Locomotive Causerie' series. My first footplate journeys were made in response from a commission in *The Engineer* to write up the workings of the newly rebuilt 'Royal Scot' 4-6-0s of the LMS some of which had been put on to running the Midland Scotch Expresses on a double-home basis between Leeds and Glasgow St Enoch. In 1945 the war was still in full blast and I had to arrange my trips during the Easter break from my duties at Westinghouse. Although I knew Maurice Earley well by that time it was not possible to expect him to come up to Ais Gill to take photographs of my runs, even if he could have got petrol coupons! At this distance in time I cannot remember how I came to know a professional photographer named Hubert Foster who then lived at Bingley, near to the main line. But he turned up trumps, and though he did not get further from his home base than Bell Busk he got a fine picture of us working hard up the bank between Skipton and Hellifield.

Later that year Foster came to York to take some photographs when I was footplating on a scruffy, out of condition 'A4 Pacific' that was on *The Flying Scotsman* but more appropriately to the subject of this chapter he was asked by the District Engineer at Leeds, LMS, to go with him in February 1947, to take some photographs of the appalling weather conditions that had blocked the Settle and Carlisle line completely for several weeks, to convince the Cabinet, in London, of the true state of affairs on the railways of the North. But railway photography on this most famous line really began to come into its own when my good friend the Revd Eric Treacy was demobilized from his wartime duties as a Chaplain to the Forces, and took up a living in the West Riding, from which district eventually he became Lord Bishop of Wakefield. Before the war he had made his mark on the railway photographic world, with his fine pictures on the lines around Liverpool, and then in the post-war world he naturally went to the Settle and Carlisle.

He rode on the footplate of various locomotives and took exciting photographs when hanging well out of their cabs on some of the most picturesque sections of the line. He brilliantly illustrated the relevant chapter of the first edition of my book *Main Lines Across the Border* which was published by Nelsons in 1960. At that time the motive power was entirely LMS, with some Austerity 2-8-0s on some of the freight trains. The BR 'Britannia' 4-6-2s had not penetrated thus far. But the age of motoring, was bringing more and more enthusiasts to the district and the lineside in Upper Ribblesdale, the wild sections between the north end of Blea Moor Tunnel and Ais Gill Summit were being photographed, not alas too frequently when there was dynamometer car tests of locomotives other than of LMS origin. Most of the shots taken in these circumstances were by engineers actually engaged on the testing work. Then came the time when the fate of the line itself was in the balance, and the economists of BR wished to close it down altogether. Fortunately by Government, not BR, decree this was prevented, and now the line, and its magnificent scenery, is a parade ground for many of the historic steam locomotives preserved and in main line running condition.

Today, enjoying the many photographs beautifully reproduced in colour in the popular journals of our day, as an old stager I cannot but regret that the railway photographic art was not brought to bear on the line as it was in the pre-1914 heyday of the Midland Railway. The one photograph that gave the slightest impression of the mountain grandeur to be enjoyed from the train windows between Settle and Appleby I painted in water colours, and as I have previously explained the train and its locomotives are not exactly typical to everyday working on the line prior to grouping. Nowadays there are some very fine artists working on railway subjects, but it would perhaps be too much to expect that any of them would forsake the whole impressive pageant of modern preserved power to go back eighty years and depict what the Settle and Carlisle line was like when Cecil J Allen wrote his contribution to the September 1913 issue of *The Railway Magazine* and detailed no less than thirteen runs from Hellifield to Carlisle, in which eight different types of Midland express locomotives were featured.

To excite any artists who have leanings in this direction I may add that the locomotives were as follows. The most powerful were the superheated 999 class 4-4-0s which had been upgraded to Class 4 since superheating. On the Carlisle road they seemed to be better engines than the compounds, then non-superheated, albeit designated by Derby reckoning Class 4. At the other end of the power scale were the 2-4-0s, both the outside framed Kirtleys, rebuilt with Johnson type boilers, and the Johnson 6ft. 6in. class, both used as pilots to Ais Gill. Three types of 4-4-0 were used for piloting, the 6ft. 6in. rebuilds, that were concerned in the Ais Gill accident, also the variety that had been rebuilt with a Belpaire firebox but still non-superheated, and then an original Johnson 4-4-0 nurebuilt. The 6ft. 6in. rebuilds, with parallel boilers, formed the bulk of the non-superheated train-engine motive power in the *Railway Magazine* table, though on one occasion with a very light load of less than 200 tons one of the 7ft. rebuilds was used. So, I tempt my artist friends to have a go!

Chapter 4

Lyndhurst – Cottages by Swan Green

By the end of the First World War my Uncle Fred, who for nearly twenty years had carried the important and exacting task of Town Clerk in the City of Bradford, felt it was time to retire. His tenure of office had included the establishment of the Lord Mayoralty of the City, a Royal visit by the Prince and Princess (later to become King George V and Queen Mary) and then all the hassle of an England at first unprepared for a major war on its very front door as it was. A crack shot himself he recruited several companies from the employees of the Corporation, trained them in military duties and commanded them himself with the rank of Major. Unhappily in the early spring of 1916 their only child, my beloved cousin Winnie, died at the early age of 16. My uncle and aunt could not face living in what had been a happy family house in Bradford and they moved away to a handsome villa on the outskirts of Harrogate. They were not long there, because as soon as the war was over he retired and went to live on the South Coast, first at Eastbourne and then at Bournemouth.

My own entry to Imperial College, in London, to begin my professional engineering training came soon after their move to Bournemouth and, with an open invitation to visit them at any weekend, in the four years when I was at college I saw a good deal of the country Forest-wise from Bournemouth. My uncle, although an expert motorist, did not feel inclined to go for any long trips, but each year at the start of the long summer vacation when my invitation to Bournemouth extended to a fortnight, before I went home to

23

Barrow, I took my bicycle with me and was often able to start on a morning excursion soon after breakfast. So sometimes in the company of my uncle, sometimes alone, I came to love the western ranges of the New Forest. My uncle never went much farther east than Ringwood, though he was always keen to take me up to Picket Post, that marvellous viewpoint, from which one can see very far in every direction of the compass.

In pre-war days my uncle was a keen photographer in many European countries, and he followed my efforts with interest and enthusiasm. On my sixteenth birthday my father gave me a postcard-size folding Brownie camera which was my faithful companion for upwards of thirty years, and which took landscapes, portraits, locomotives, trains in motion, and ships. My uncle was always interested in my subjects especially when I rode my bicycle to Sandown, took the little motor boat ferry across the narrow entrance to Poole Harbour and then rode several miles across the sands to Studland and then up to the summit of the fascinating Old Harry Rocks. East of Bournemouth I had many times passed in non-stopping trains between Southampton and Bournemouth the station of Lyndhurst Road, but the little town, in the Forest, was several miles away, and eventually I got there by push-bike. There I was charmed by the lovely cottages around Swan Green and I took many photographs of them. Like my uncle I did all my own processing at first, and my films had to wait until I got up to my parents' house in Barrow to use the jury-rigged dark room in the bathroom upstairs. The Lyndhurst pictures turned out well and I was fascinated by the way the texture of the cottage buildings were rendered in monochrome. I was still at Imperial College at the time and still had long holidays; I had managed to carry the beautiful tones of the antique brickwork of those cottages in my mind and I painted the scene in water colours.

As usual I outlined the main shape of the building in light pencil, but while I certainly had in mind the colour of the brickwork of those cottages in view of the lapse of time before I had actually seen them and coming to commit them to a watercolour painting I thought it advisable to do some checking up. My father had in his library at Barrow two books that I thought might be helpful. The first was one of those beautiful creations of the pre-war world of publish-

Lyndhurst, in the New Forest: thatched cottages on Swan Green.

ing, a volume called simply 'Hampshire', in the series of gorgeous colour-books by A & C Black. The artist was Wilfred Ball, with whose work I was already familiar, in an equally delightful book on 'Sussex' in the same series. But while in 'Hampshire' there were many colour plates rendering in faithful detail the features of cottages of all shapes and sizes, most of them with thatched roofs in a glorious variety of styles, and states of repair, the building rarely showed the basic brickwork. It seemed to have been painted over to give an appearance of creamy yellow – very pretty, but not what I was looking for. In the chapter dealing with the New Forest there were no paintings of cottages of any kind. So I turned to the second book.

This was called 'The New Forest', but by a different writer and artist, and a different publisher. It also was a pre-war book, and the 50-odd colour plates, though of a different style to those of Wilfred Ball were equally delightful. They included one, indeed, of Swan Green Lyndhurst, where my photograph had been taken, but unfortunately not including the actual cottages that I wished to paint. However this, and other pictures in this book, gave me the lead I was looking for, and the picture was duly painted. My father had the result framed and hung on one of the walls in our house at Barrow. Reverting to my father in my leisured moments, which are becoming increasingly frequent with advancing years, I read through the book on 'The New Forest' with renewed interest. In his younger days my father was a great reader, and with any subject with which he was particularly interested he made carefully phrased pencil notes in the margin, of topics on which he had pronounced views. Unlike his elder brother, who was as much a bookworm as he was, and who made his side comments in ink(!), my father always had the ultimate market value of any books he bought constantly in mind so his own asides or downright condemnations were always carefully written lightly, with a specially soft pencil.

One gathers nowadays, sixty or more years since he visited the New Forest with my Uncle Fred, that he was not very impressed with the author's literary style, however much he admired the pictures. On the side of the painting of Bucklers Hard, on the Beaulieu River leading down to the Solent, he had pencilled in that he had tea in one of the cottages there, and viewed some rare manuscripts from royal celebrities. This note concluded: 'not even mentioned by author'. This obviously was a passing comment, because when he reached the end of the book he delivered this broadside: 'To leave out any mention of Bucklers Hard shows that the writer had no liking of such places but was merely a botanist and copier of beautiful and musty records.' My father wrote on: 'It was a place of national importance, to make ships here, built the old battleships . . .'

Dipping into another of my father's books 'Highways and Byways of Hampshire' I found, noted in pencil, that four of the wooden-wall battleships that formed part of Nelson's triumphant fleet at the Battle of Trafalgar were built at Bucklers Hard, namely the *Agamemnon*, the *Euryalus*, the *Illustrious* and the *Swiftsure*. I must admit that all four names became familiar to me, not as those of wooden-wall battleships built at Bucklers Hard, but as express locomotives built by the London and North Western Railway at Crewe!

I did not go to Lyndhurst for several years after I painted that picture, and then I went there almost by accident. I had been in Le Havre on business and was intending to return by the Saturday night packet steamer to Southampton. Some good friends of mine from my earlier amateur theatrical days had gone to live in the village of Whiteparish, northwards from Southampton, and I had a standing invitation to call on them any time I was in the district. They met me off the boat that Sunday morning and took me to their home, travelling, I was very pleased to find, via Lyndhurst. Swan Green in its autumn colours looked lovelier than ever. I spent a delightful day with my friends at Whiteparish, and then caught the Pullman *Bournemouth Belle* back to London. On the journey back I did some quiet thinking. When I was in the London office of Westinghouse as a draughtsman one of my favourite lunch-time haunts was the Georgian Tea Room on Kings Cross Station where one or other of the attractively styled waitresses brought me buns or sandwiches, or whatever my then frugal tastes might be. Soon one of my favourites among the girls was promoted to be a counterhand, and I had more opportunities of chatting her up. I then discovered we had a keen mutual interest in the beauties of the countryside, and one day, greatly daring, I asked her if she had ever been to the New Forest, and if she would like me to take her one Sunday. She agreed, and so

we set off from Waterloo, again on *The Bournemouth Belle*, for Southampton.

We took the bus to Lyndhurst and I was thrilled to see how she
obviously loved all she saw from the cottages on Swan Green, to the
beautiful woodlands where we walked, to the wide prospects from
Emery Down. It was a lovely day, and before we got back to London it
seemed that we had plighted our troth! Some months went by before
our formal engagement was announced but before then there came
an incident that even now causes me to chuckle when I recall it. It
was the first occasion when I brought Olivia to meet my family in
their home where I lived for some years at Bushey. It was not exactly
a formal occasion though my mother, as was her wont, was a trifle
upstage throughout. She was one of the Patrician-like women who
felt that no other woman was good enough for her son! It was slightly
embarrassing for me when I brought some of my amateur theatrical
girl friends to the house. My introduction of Olivia went well
enough, or so I thought, and when I had taken her down to the
station to catch a late evening train back to London I came back to
find the rest of my family in intimate conclave. At my entrance it was
my sister who spoke first. 'Well,' she said, 'we've had a committee
meeting, and she'll do!' I think I can have been very restrained not
to burst out with hearty laughter seeing that we'd made up our own
minds about six months previously! Our formal engagement came
soon afterwards.

That same Autumn we were in the New Forest again enjoying the
glades near Lyndhurst in all the glory of their exquisite colouring,
but in the following April we were on *The Bournemouth Belle* for a single trip only. Uncle Fred was coming up to Bushey for our wedding
and as the road journey was more than he was content to make solo,
he then being well over seventy, Olivia and I went to Bournemouth
to accompany him. He was still an excellent driver, but we all
thought he should have company on a long journey. It proved a
delightful trip, picnicking on the way in the New Forest near one of
his own favourite haunts, Stoney Cross. It was not until after World
War II that I visited the district again, then in overalls in the course
of some footplate journeys on Southern Railway locomotives. Then,
for almost fifty years Lyndhurst and the cottages around Swan Green

remained nothing more than a memory kept alive by the picture I had painted fully seventy years ago, and on which the colours were still surprisingly fresh. Then one day a dear friend sent me a post-card, of the very scene I had painted. She thought I would like to see how it was now. The cottages were still there but horribly modern-ized, though probably much more hygienic to live in! The brickwork had been painted over, and was much the same colour as some of the cottages painted by Wilfrid Ball.

Chapter 5

Torbay – Monument to the Prince of Orange at Brixham

This chapter could well be classified as an essay in English history, seeing the focal point of the piece commemorates a dramatic event in the time of the House of Stuart, in the seventeenth century. The trouble really started with Union of the thrones of England and Scotland and the accession of King James I. The Stuarts were Roman Catholics and, while he and his son did not attempt to impose their faith on the English people, Charles I stirred up enough trouble in other directions to provoke the Civil War, and eventually his public execution at the hands of Oliver Cromwell. But the extremes of Puritanism imposed on the country by the victors in the Civil War were palling on much of the population even before the death of Cromwell, and the restoration of the Stuart Kings under the gay Charles II let loose a brief era of unrestrained personal behaviour by rich and poor alike that was the immediate opposite of the Puritanism that had preceded it. With the accession of James II all seemed set for the imposition of the Catholic faith as the basic religion of Great Britain, but this time opposition took a more subtle way than outright military rebellion.

The handsome but headstrong Charles I had three children. The two sons eventually succeeded him as Charles II and James II of England, but his daughter Mary married the staunchly protestant Prince of Orange and of course lived in the Netherlands. They had a son who married Mary, eldest daughter of James II. The anti-Catholic faction, which undoubtedly constituted the large majority of

29

responsible opinion in England, had been in close liaison with the Prince of Orange, twice allied by marriage to the House of Stuart, and in 1688 they invited him come over and assume the British Throne. With his lady wife, daughter of James II, another link with the Stuarts, they were accepted as 'William and Mary', joint sovereigns of the United Kingdom. But before continuing the story of how I came to paint the statue erected on the quay in Brixham harbour I must tell of two other naval occasions in Torbay.

When we arrived at Paignton in July 1925, on a Friday afternoon, we found all Torbay agog in anticipation of the arrival, on a summer cruise, of a squadron of light cruisers of the Royal Navy and some attendant destroyers. They were arriving on the first Saturday morning, so I took the road to seek out some advantageous points for railway photography. When I got back for midday lunch the fleet had arrived, and a magnificent spectacle they presented. The weather was gloriously fine and calm, and on that Saturday afternoon, I scouted round finding out places where one could hire rowing boats. On Sunday morning with my father as passenger I set off from Paignton beach and rowed out to where the ships were anchored. As will well be imagined there were numerous other craft around: motor launches bringing parties intent on taking advantage of the hospitality of certain ships in welcoming visitors. But I was keen on photographing from the waterline, as it were, and I rowed my father round until I had exposed all six of the roll of postcard-size film that I had taken out with me. The weather continued perfect and the pictures turned out well. I was very sorry to learn, after the Second World War had been raging for some time, that some of the ships I photographed that day had been lost, by enemy action.

Almost one hundred and twelve years before my own visit there had been another naval occasion in Torbay which was of deep historical significance. In 1815 the great wooden-walled battleship *Bellerophon* anchored in the bay. She was carrying Napoleon Bonaparte after his defeat in the Battle of Waterloo and subsequent capture by the British Army. In HMS *Bellerophon* he was in an early stage of his journey to the South Atlantic island of St Helena, where he was to be held in captivity for the rest of his life. In the very anxious days of 1940, when there was a real threat of a German invasion of England, I shall always remember a cartoon showing Hitler poised on the cliffs between Boulogne and Calais looking expectantly across the Straits of Dover, and beside him was the ghost of Napoleon saying 'Yes, I got this far too Adolf!' Actually Napoleon got a good deal nearer to our shores, than a distant look across the Straits of Dover. While the *Bellerophon* was anchored in Torbay he viewed the beautiful country at a time when the now large and popular resort of Torquay was little more than a hamlet near what is left of Torre abbey. He is reputed to have exclaimed: 'Un beau pays!'

There is one more naval occasion to write about before we take the road over the hills from Paignton into Brixham. Soon after the Second World War when Olivia and I took our young children for seaside holidays at Teignmouth, we paid a visit to Torquay, by train in those days when it was so cheap. On that day I was surprised and very pleased to see one of the latest British battleships at anchor in the bay. It was one of the class built during the war, but at this distance in time I cannot remember its name. How I got near enough to it to take an almost broadside view, the resulting image taking up the full width of the postcard-size Brownie camera I was then using, I cannot remember. It was one of the last super-capital ships to be built for the Royal Navy and finding a good print of the photograph recently I showed to several of my naval friends who live near but none of them could pinpoint the few distinctive features to be able to give a name. The consensus of opinion was that it might have been the *Anson* or the *Howe*. Apropos of the names of battleships, particularly of the one in which Napoleon was conveyed to St Helena, my father sometimes mentioned an amusing perversion of the name – the *Billy-Ruffian*!

So to Brixham; I had read previously of the picturesque sight of the brown-red sails of the fishing trawlers of Brixham plying their craft in the bay, and while intent at first on warship photography I could not help seeing a positive 'armada' of ships going and coming from where I thought Brixham harbour lay. In her beautiful book lady Northcote writes: '. . . standing back within the bay is the small and pretty town of Brixham – celebrated for its trawlers, and for being the landing place of William III. The red and brown sails of "Brixham trawlers" scattered over the blue-grey waters of the bay seem very familiar, and it is a question for consideration how many exhibitions at the Royal Academy have *not* included a picture bearing that title.' Pedalling down the hill from the railway junction I made straight for the harbour, and with plenty of films in my pocket went mad in exposing picture after picture, as the red-sailed trawlers grouped themselves in fascinating formations, or so it seemed. The only trouble was that in 1925 I had no colour. I recall painting one of the pictures in water colour, but I do not know what became of it. In Lady Northcote's book there is a colour plate entitled 'Brixham Trawlers', but unfortunately, to my mind, it is one of the least satisfactory of all the plates in that book. Two of the pencil drawings reproduced in the 'Highways and Byways in Devon and Cornwall' show a fine congregation of fishing craft, but unfortunately not in colour.

Then, of course, I photographed the statue of the Prince of Orange. From another of my books I was surprised to learn that this had not been erected until 1888. This author says it is not at all what one would expect from a sculptor of that period. He writes: 'It is bold and impressionistic – his hawk eyes amazingly well delineated. There the Dutchman stands, looking as pompous as he can breath . . .' In her book Lady Northcote quotes a contemporary author's account of the landing, and as it is revealing and amusing I am re-quoting myself: 'The morning was very obscure with the Fog and Mist, and withal it was so calm that the Vessels now as it were touched each other, every ship coming as near unto the ship where in the Prince of Orange was, as the Skipper thereof would permit them.

'His Highness the Prince of Orange gave orders that his Standard should be put up, and accordingly it was done, the White Flag being put uppermost, signifying his most gracious offers of peace unto all such as would live peacefully. And under that the Red or Bloody Flag was set up, signifying War unto all such as did oppose his designs. The Sun, recovering strength, soon dissipated the fog, and dispersed the Mist, in as much that it prov'd a very pleasant day. By this time the people of Devonside thereabout had discovered the Fleet, the one telling the other thereof; they came flocking in droves to the side or brow of the Hills to view us. Some guessed we were French because they saw divers White Flags; but the standard of the Prince,

Brixham, Torbay: monument to William Prince of Orange who landed there in 1689, shortly before he and his wife, Mary, daughter of the deposed King James II, were proclaimed joint sovereigns of the United Kingdom.

the motto of which was "For the Protestant Religion and Liberty",
soon undeceived them – Bells were ringing as we sailed towards the
Bay, and as we landed, which many judged to be a good omen. A
little later, when they had landed, people came running out at their
doors to see this happy sight. So the Prince and Marshal Schomberg,
and divers Lords, Knights and Gentlemen, marched up the Hill,
which all the Fleet could see over the houses, the colours flying and
flourishing before his Highness, the Trumpets sounding the Haut-
boys played, the Drums beat . . . and so on, and so on!'

After photographing the statue, it was almost a year later that I
painted the scene in water colours. I recalled that the day in question
had been gloriously fine and in my painting I rendered the limpid
blue sky in that pigment that used to be called cobalt-blue. No other
treatment was necessary. The result was satisfying enough and the
picture hung in our home at Barrow, afterwards at Bushey until I got
married. Then, with subsequent upheaval the picture itself escaped
from my immediate notice until I came to hang it in the new house
we had purchased in Batheaston. When we came to Bath in 1948 we
had bought a massive yet very elegant Georgian house that was much
too big for our immediate needs, but believe it or not, was almost as
cheap as some of the poorly built houses that were more nearly the
accommodation we then needed. In our new house, 'Silver Cedars', I
was rather horrified to find that the 'limpid' blue skies above the
Prince of Orange statue had turned to a pale fawn! My first thought
was to take the picture out of the frame and repaint the sky, but
more immediate jobs in our new house awaited me and the intention
lapsed. Then I remembered having seen one of my father's books
containing colour plates of reproductions of historic water colours,
that not only were the skies faded beyond recognition, from the
original colour but most of the rest of the pictures were very much
faded. So my William of Orange remains in the ranks of the 'old
masters' of water-colours!

Very many years later when Olivia and I with our six-footer Trevor,
paid a visit to Torbay I photographed the statue in colour and what a
difference it made, with the blue sky overhead and the animated
harbour scene in the background. Gone alas were the brown sails of
the trawlers and there was another difference to be noted – not until

I got home and had the colour film processed did I realize what this difference was. The railings round the statue, which I painted faithfully from my 1925 photograph, had gone and on the southside of the monument was a seat on which two middle-aged matrons were sitting. I took a colour photograph with Olivia and Trevor sitting on the stones, which in 1925 would, of course, be out of reach.

Chapter 6
York Minster – Bootham Bar

I was first taken to the City of York, and to see its magnificent Minster in the early summer of 1916, when I was only eleven years old. The circumstances were somewhat unusual. Earlier in that same year my father's place of business had been transferred from Reading to Barrow-in-Furness, and the family home was in the process of being set up in a smart semi-detached villa on the outskirts of that northern town. While my mother was getting the house more or less to her liking my young sister and I were taken to the new house in Harrogate to which my Uncle Fred and Aunt Emmie had gone, from Central Bradford after the rather tragic death of my cousin earlier that year. My mother took us by train from Furness Abbey to Skipton where my Aunt, with her gardener-chauffeur was waiting with their car, to take us children over the moors to Harrogate.

My uncle was very keen that we should have a proper introduction to the North Country, and although he himself was still very much in business at the time and could not take time off to accompany us he was keen for us to be shown around and one such trip he recommended was to York. The gardener-chauffeur was available and Auntie Emma was as always a charming cicerone. So one fine summer day we set out from Harrogate to York. I don't remember much of that motor ride. Presumably we passed through Knaresborough, but that picturesque little town evidently made no impression in my mind at the time. I was more impressed with the very flat and level country through which we passed, in such contrast to the wild hilly moorlands we had traversed on our way to Harrogate from Skipton. I was not to know then that Knaresborough had first been reached

35

from York by a railway only 15 miles long with the grandiose title
'East and West Yorkshire Junction Railway', not entirely at first,
because at its western end the bridge carrying the line over the River
Nidd into the town itself collapsed and had to be rebuilt. The new
version opened in 1851 was the monumental structure with castel-
lated copings which safely carries even the modern 'Pacific' engines
on the steam hauled special trains of today.

When we reached York my aunt had no thoughts but for the
Minster, and we were escorted round by an enthusiastic young man.
At this long distance in time I cannot remember if he was a clergyman or not. I remember being very impressed with the celebrated
'Five Sisters' window, though I must confess to having to look up its
significance again in one of my own books recently before writing
these lines. Our guide was keen that we should complete our tour of
the magnificent cathedral by climbing up inside one of the West
towers and enjoying the view over the city. My eight-year-old sister
and I hesitated at this suggestion, but the irrepressible young man
said at once 'you can go up with this young lady'. My aunt retorted:
'Young lady, I am an old woman!!' Although then nearing the age of
sixty she was still very beautiful and had kept a trim figure; but
physical jerks had never been one of her accomplishments, and to
climb the ladders inside of one of the west towers of York Minster was
not the place in which to begin!

I cannot remember how my sister and I travelled from Harrogate
to our new home in Barrow. I imagined our mother came for us and
took us by train all the way, but I have no recollections of that
journey, except that we went through some long tunnels on the way.
From our days at the Bank house in central Reading I had always
been an avid collector of coloured railway postcards and with my
even-then photographic memory I remembered I had a picture of a
North Eastern Train coming out of 'Bramhope Tunnel'. I had then
no idea where this was. The postcard itself gave no clue except the
engine was a large 4-4-0. But then no more than some nine months
were to elapse before I went to stay with my uncle and my aunt again
in Harrogate. It was the time of the Easter holiday. My young sister
was down with the flu, and my mother, afraid of my catching it when
I came home for the school holidays, arranged for me to go to

Harrogate for a week or so. There was no question of a car from Skipton this time. It was by train all the way, but at first I was in the company of some boys whose homes were in the West Riding of Yorkshire. From Leeds onwards I was on my own.

From the age of about seven or eight years I had been accustomed to travelling on my own between Mortimer and Reading, and at Leeds I quickly found my way from the Midland station to the adjacent one of the North Eastern, from which I had to travel to Harrogate. In the meantime, thinking of the picture-postcard, I had made some enquiries among my new friends at Giggleswick School as to where Bramhope was, and I was interested to find it as the name of a small village not five miles north of where one family lived on the northern outskirts of Leeds. The long tunnel in which I had previously travelled was obviously that under the high moorland on which the present Leeds and Bradford Airport is sited. But the local train in which I found myself apparently started the wrong way! When boarding the train I did not notice where the engine was, and on leaving Leeds we were heading eastwards. Fortunately for my peace of mind it was an all-stations 'stopper', and in the manner of local railway workings in those days the porters on the stations yelled the destination of the train at each stop. It was taking the alternative route to Harrogate, via Wetherby, one that has been closed for some time, although still having its route marked on the latest one-inch Ordnance Survey Map.

On this visit we did not travel far. The year was 1917 and my uncle was very busy, not only with municipal affairs concerning the City of Bradford, but also in his wartime service as commanding officer of the company of city council employees which he had recruited and trained as a volunteer defence force. My next visit to York came four years later, in somewhat different circumstances. In the Easter holidays of 1921 I was staying at the home of my good friend John Moore. Nearly five years earlier we had been new boys at Giggleswick School. For the intervening years we had been in the same form and then at midsummer we would both be leaving. Ever since those school days we have been close friends. John was two years older than I, and in my own advanced age I still keep in touch with his widow. But reverting to 1921 I had my bicycle with me in Leeds, and from his home in Chapel Allerton we made numerous excursions. One day John suggested a trip to York. His father intervened and said if we were proposing to go that far Fountains Abbey was a far more attractive place; but then John said, 'We want to see some engines, and there will be lots of them at York.' So, provided with a handsome packed lunch, we set out. But we soon found that York station and its immediate environs was not exactly a place for two enthusiastic train spotters, encumbered with push-bicycles; neither were the train windows of excessively crowded Saturday services on which I was taken with my family between Leeds and Whitby in the following summer.

It was not until Christmas of 1924 that York came into the family picture again, and then by the receipt of a sumptuous box of Rowntree's chocolates. I have no doubt that the contents of that box were delicious, but it was the picture on the lid of that box that really took my fancy. It was a reproduction of a painting of one of the old gates of the City, Bootham Bar, with the towers of York Minster seen in the background. It was a beautiful composition, and as soon as the contents of that box had been devoured I asked for the lid and put it in my archives. There was no time to do anything about it in the time remaining before I had to go back to London for further studies, at Imperial College, but at Easter I got to work on a water-colour of the scene. The trouble was, however, I had never been in that part of York myself. The artist who had painted the original picture obviously portrayed the scene as he knew it, before the tram lines were installed, and the people looked mid-Victorian in their dress. I painted the scene in my own style, and it was not until several years later that I visited the site and saw how things had changed, not of course to Bootham Bar itself, which I have since realized is one of the most attractive of the old entrance gates to the City, with the Minster rising majestically behind it.

In those early days most of my visits to York were no more than brief overnight stays when travelling farther afield, with no more than cheap bed and breakfast accommodation; but I always took my drawing of Bootham Bar, then unframed, with me to check up points. In due course as I climbed higher in the Westinghouse hierarchy, and business brought important contracts for new signalling work in the North-Eastern Area of the LNER, with which I became

York, before the electric tramway system was installed. One of the medieval gates of the city, Bootham Bar, with the towers of the Minster rising behind.

deeply involved, my visits to York greatly increased, particularly as my contacts with the technical journals of the Tothill Press led to my being awarded important commissions for writing up lengthy descriptions of what was going on. My stays in York became considerably longer than hurried overnight visits, and increasingly close friendship with the railway engineers with whom I was associated led to some delightful social occasions, from which I learned a great deal more about the great historic City of York than could be culled from the ordinary guide books.

I walked round the medieval city walls and found the circuit, although not complete in its preservation, included no more than a few gaps, indeed the finest and most spectacular length is opposite the main railway station. But I have often wondered over the outcry the preservationists of the early 1830s might have raised when the engineers of the York and North Midland Railway, as it then was, bored a hole through that medieval wall to gain access to what was to be their principal terminal station! To do the engineers every credit they made a very handsome tunnel in the wall, where carriage sidings now stand, and the wall extends not far to the east to Micklegate Bar striding across one of the main highways into the city from the south. I found also Monkgate Bar and Walmsgate Bar, the latter still having the medieval barbican at the entrance. Having seen the other three, and photographed them I am sure that Bootham Bar, which I had painted before I had even seen it 'in the flesh', as it were, was the most picturesque of them all, notably from having a fine Norman arch over the roadway. At one time Micklegate Bar lay very close to another of my places of interest in York, the Railway Museum. But I must steer clear of historic railway interests just now!

I must have led my inherent interest in railways to end my walk along this southern arm of the city walls at Micklegate Bar, because I then missed completely one of the most important medieval sights – the scant ruins of the once-magnificent St Mary's Abbey. It was not till very many years later that I learned of their existence, and then only on perusing an old book that my father bequeathed to me after his death at the age of 84 years. The book, published in 1908, was entitled 'The Greater Abbeys of England' and contained 61 beautifully painted colour plates, though I was surprised to find that Bath

Abbey was not included. It was not until a recent study of the book that I realized what a fascinating relic I had missed completely. It was charmingly painted in one of the magnificent collections in that now much treasured book. The book somewhat naturally contained no references to the episodes in the history of the City of York with which I myself became involved from the year 1957 onwards. Then I had been commissioned to write a book about the Railway Races to the North that took place in 1888 and 1895, and in studying contemporary reports before beginning my own writing I found that in 1888 at any rate York played a somewhat significant part, so far as some travellers were concerned.

In the very first issue of *The Railway Magazine*, published in July 1897 there was the first of a three-instalment article by a clergyman, the Revd W J Scott, entitled 'Some Racing Runs and Trial Trips'. Scott was an advanced Anglo-Catholic, and already one of the band of intellectual railway enthusiasts. He was something of a stylist in his writing, as the following extract from his inaugural piece in *The Railway Magazine* shows. In 1888 there were no restaurant cars on the Scottish expresses, and the 10 a.m. from Kings Cross waited at York for twenty minutes while the passengers made a dash for the refreshment room. Presumably Scott had his own means of sustenance, for he writes:

'We turn our steps towards the city. For the most part, towns on the Continent are more picturesque and interesting than those in England, though the country in Britain is far more beautiful than any we find across the Channel; but York can hold its own for quaintness and grandeur with almost any town of like size in Europe. Under a bright midday sun, the old city with its girdling walls and crown of towers looked very beautiful: despite some stir of life, and the jingle of tram-cars, it seemed very still, its river slipping by as great emperor Constantine saw it glide in the self same channel, lapping the walls of houses that stood where the houses one looks at from Lendal Bridge or Ousegate Bridge stand today. Never a "buried city": a Roman capital, a chief city of the North England kingdom, and of the kindred Danes which over ran that kingdom; a seat of Government, the "Council of the North" in medieval days, and now metropolis of Northern England (though the Scottish Lowlands have thrown off the yoke of the English primate), and a railway capital behind London alone in importance, Elboracum, Eoforwic, Iorvik, York, in the year AD 200 or the year 1890, from Severus and Paulinus to Dr Maclagan – and should we say George S Gibb – she still "sits a queen". Only three and a half hours from London; but how utterly unlike London is the tongue one hears spoken – that strong, if sometimes rough, North English, which Southerners always call "Scotch", though at least five English shires share it with the Lowlands across the border. In the garden of the toll-house of "Lendall Bridge" – since done away with – a small boy is trying in vain to catch a white rabbit. "Tak' it up by lugs, bairn, tak' 't up by lugs!" cried his elder brother, much to the bewilderment of a tourist from the South who stands listening. But it is time to turn back to the station.'

I should add that George S Gibb was then General Manager of the North Eastern Railway, with whom Scott was very friendly, but I have no idea who Dr Maclagan was. The railway authorities at York seemed to have some classical learnings amongst them, because one of the main line signal boxes was named 'Severus Junction' after the Roman Emperor who died in the city. One of my own last visits to York was in motoring days, when my dear wife and I had a charming lady companion who had been a family friend for very many years. We had come up via Lincoln and on the morning after our arrival we took our visitor to see some of the sights. After making due obeisance to the glories of the Minster we took her to Bootham Bar. It was many years since the tram lines had been removed, but on a summer Saturday morning the place was teeming, with traffic pouring into the City Centre through that medieval archway. My thoughts were inevitably directed to the painting on one of my walls at home!

Chapter 7
Tebay Troughs – The 'Up Corridor'

I was still at school at Giggleswick when my father, appreciating my increasing interest in the London and North Western Railway, gave me a bound volume of certain back numbers of *The Railway Magazine* which contained the first instalments of the famous series of historic articles 'Locomotive and Train Working in the latter part of the Nineteenth Century', by E L Ahrons. The first instalment dealt with the London and North Western Railway. I read these and was fascinated, but in this same volume were some very interesting accounts of express train running over the route between Crewe and Carlisle. On my journeys to and from school, when we always had to change from the Furness to the Midland trains at Carnforth, I used to see the London and North Western Anglo-Scottish expresses passing through, often at a seemingly high speed, and in the pages of *The Railway Magazine* I learned of the way they continued through the Westmoreland fell country to Carlisle. At Giggleswick, and excursions therefrom, I had become very much aware of what the fell country was like, though I was later to appreciate that the country through which the London and North Western had to force its way to get to Carlisle was very different from the limestone dales through which the Midland Railway ran.

That volume of *The Railway Magazine* contained only one illustration of a London and North Western train in the hill country and this is not a very enlightening picture. The ace moving train photographer of those days, F E Mackay, who I came to know well in my

42

student days at Imperial College, was not very pictorially minded. He concentrated in getting a close-up shot of the engine and train in motion, and this he did very successfully. He sought out locations where trains were picking up water at speed, and one of these was just south of the moorland junction of Tebay, in the heart of the wildest fell country. The troughs in any case had to be installed on level track, and there was only one place in the sixty-old miles south from Carlisle until the line reached almost level ground by the shores of Morecambe Bay. Those troughs in the high fell country were a great help to enginemen of southbound express trains, the engines of which had been worked hard up the almost continuous climb from Carlisle to Shap Summit at an altitude of 915 ft. above sea level, only 31½ miles from the start. The water supply in the tender would have been much depleted by this continuous hard work. The London and North Western Railway was very generous in its provision of water troughs. They had many long non-stop runs by the principal express trains and the tenders fitted to the locomotives were not very large.

South of Carnforth the provision of two more sets of water troughs in the 27 miles between that junction and Preston might seem unduly lavish. These were at Hest Bank, right near the shores of Morecambe Bay, 3 miles from Carnforth, and at Brock, 8 miles north of Preston. In the early 1900s many of the Anglo-Scottish expresses, both by day and night, were timed to run the 141 miles between Crewe and Carlisle without any intermediate stops. Usually these fast trains were heavily loaded and required two engines. With both engines requiring water it was a case of some contrivance and co-operation between the engine crews, and the provision of two sets of troughs only about fifteen miles apart, as at Brock and Hest Bank, enabled the crews on a double-headed train each to get a really good fill-up before coming to the heavy climbing to the Shap Summit. Then, if either engine was a little short of water, after the first pull, up to Grayrigg, there was another set of troughs before Tebay.

Picking up water at speed could be a most spectacular sight to photograph, because the troughs were located on fast-running sections of the lines. Mackay frequented the troughs at Wiske Moor, on the North Eastern, north of Northallerton, those on the Lancashire and Yorkshire west of Manchester, and on the London and North Western at Bushey, near Watford. In his early days he never worked at Hest Bank, and I did not see many shots of his at Tebay. On one of my own first visits to the latter place a southbound express had come down the Shap incline at such a pace as to pass through Tebay station at fully 80 m.p.h., and when no more than half a mile later on the fireman lowered the scoop to pick up water the spray completely enveloped the leading coaches of the train! On the North Western I have seen photographs of double-headed trains where the tender tank of the leading engine was overflowing to such an extent that the train engine was completely obliterated, and the picture looked as though there was a light engine running on its own and a train of carriages emerging from the clouds of spray some distance in the rear.

But water troughs or not it was the magnificent scenery that held me spellbound, as the saying goes, when I first saw the fells that bordered the gorge of the river Lune when the Grayrigg summit was passed and the main line dipped down to the moorland junction of Low Gill. In the turbulent railway politics of the 1870s this remote location could easily have become a main line junction of the first importance. Certain interests were intent in promoting an entry to Scotland by the Midland Railway, before the famous Settle and Carlisle line was even proposed, let alone surveyed and built. There was an offshoot of the Midland, called the Little North Western running north-westwards from Skipton and this had a branch to Ingleton. The Lancaster and Carlisle Railway, which was then independent but closely associated with the London and North Western, decided to build a line southwards from Low Gill to link up with the Midland branch at Ingleton, and moreover build it as a first class mainline, capable of carrying the heaviest locomotives. When the Midland built the Settle and Carlisle line its usefulness diminished and it became a merely sparsely-used branch line, and in the 1960s abandoned completely. I am glad, however, to have a record of an express run over it, made by a special train, *The Three Summits Tour*, in 1963, made when we had travelled south from Carlisle, over Shap, and then took the Ingleton line at Low Gill. Appropriately to the construction standards of the branch line we had a Gresley streamlined 'A4' Pacific to haul us.

Railway politics apart, and apart from all considerations of railway engineering, the country through which the main line of the London and North Western Railway runs north of Low Gill is magnificent in the great hills that tower on both sides of the line. I found it evident that Mackay, and other expert photographers who had worked in this area, had little eye for the scenic background to the trains they took, but fortunately while the London, and North Western Railway was still un-grouped I was given a walking pass to photograph on the line between Low Gill and Tebay, and I spent some happy days, finding new places and new backgrounds, at which to photograph the many express trains that were scheduled over the line in those far-off days. How I remember the midday procession south from Carlisle:

> Edinburgh to Euston (with a coach for Birmingham)
> Glasgow to Euston (with a coach for Birmingham, and a Great Western one for Plymouth)
> Glasgow and Edinburgh to Manchester and Liverpool
> Aberdeen and Dundee to London Euston

The second and third of the trains in the above succession were usually double-headed in the height of the summer season, so there were six engines to 'spot' even in this one group of trains. There was greater activity on the down main line around three o'clock in the afternoon. First came the midday departures from Liverpool and Manchester, and then the two sections of the 10 a.m. from Euston, which in LMS days were coupled together and named *The Royal Scot*. One day when I was photographing at Tebay a diverting incident befell the first of the London trains. Long before the days when traffic working on this route was regulated by the train control system, introduced on the Midland Railway in the pre-war years and subsequently adopted over the whole of the LMS, the signalman at Low Gill sent a slow goods northwards after the Liverpool and Manchester train had passed. It made slow progress, and was no more than ambling along when it passed me, in position to photograph the first of the London trains. Down the valley I could see that this latter train, double-headed, was being brought almost to a stand at Dillicar intermediate signals. The signal cleared just in time to avoid stopping the express.

Two miles farther on, as they neared my position, they were going 'flat-out' to work up speed before they reached the heavy approach gradients of the Shap Incline itself, and gave me a superb smoke effect. The picture I secured afterwards formed the colour frontispiece of one of my later books. It was worked into a beautiful picture of 'period' LNWR working by the artist Victor Welch, who was working for Ian Allan at that time. The Edinburgh section of the train came about ten minutes later running under clear signals. It was hauled by the pioneer LNWR four cylinder of 4-6-0, the *Sir Gilbert Claughton*, and I secured another of what became my favourite train photographs. After that I walked back to Tebay station and motive power yard, and took some photographs of the bank engines used to assisting trains up the Shap Incline. By that time in the long day I had used up all the films I had brought with me, and while waiting for the local train which would take me to Oxenholme, and there I would change for the Furness train for Grange-over-Sands, I looked out for the two up Anglo-Scottish expresses which had left Glasgow and Edinburgh at 1.30 p.m. Both trains carried portions for London, Liverpool and Manchester and at Symington, they were remarshalled, the London coaches making up the stock of the southbound 'Corridor'. The famous nickname of this most prestigious of Anglo-Scottish expresses dates from the 1890s when the train was one of the first ever in Great Britain to be corridor throughout.

On the station platform at Tebay I saw the signals lowered for it to pass, and then it came from the approach gradients at the foot of the Shap Incline, running at about 70 m.p.h. headed by one of the 'Claughton' class 4-6-0 and hauling a rake of those palatial 12-wheeled corridor coaches, built by the LNWR specially for this service, and still used well into LMS days on the train which then became known as 'The Midday Scot'. After the train had passed on this very much pre-LMS occasion I could not help recalling the complete absence of any colour plates of the famous train, on the North Western part of the journey, in the illustrated magazine dealing with railway subjects. Mackay photographed the northbound train frequently in the London area, but in the north, with the up train, most of his shots were taken on the Caledonian line north of Carlisle. One of these with the beautiful blue 4-6-0 *Cardean* was cer-

In the Lune Gorge, in LNWR days, the southbound 'Corridor' express, Glasgow and Edinburgh to London picking up water from Tebay troughs at 70 m.p.h.

tainly made the subject of a handsome colour plate in *The Railway Magazine*, but never a sign of one leaving Carlisle for the south with a gleaming black North Western engine on the job. The only coloured picture that I can recall of 'The Corridor' is a Rapheal-Tuck postcard, stylishly drawn but not all that accurate, taken from an official photograph of the down train taken near Wolverton and used in monochrome, frequently afterwards in railway publicity papers and leaflets.

On my homeward journey that evening, in the three successive stages, Tebay to Oxenholme, Oxenholme to Grange-over-Sands, and thence to Furness Abbey, while munching the rest of the generous supply of sandwiches that my mother had provided for a long day's sustenance, I thought deeply about the lack of colour plates of the 'Up Corridor' and though time was running short in the particular college vacation I was then enjoying I determined to paint a picture of my own. In *The Railway Magazine* of April 1915 there was a good Mackay picture of a 'Claughton', on Tebay troughs, not hauling the up 'Corridor' but a semi-local train, I took it as a guide and sketched out in pencil the outlines of the picture. I finished it in the Christmas holidays, and my father had it framed. It hung on one of the walls of my private 'den' on the top floor of the big house in Bushey where the family lived after my father's retirement from business. It remained there until I got married and then, due to lack of space, it was consigned to a cupboard. There it remained until we bought our first post-war house on Sion Hill Bath, where there was plenty of wall space.

Then, some thirty years later. I was approached by the publishing firm Michael Joseph to collaborate in the production of a sumptuous book they were planning to be called 'The Railway Heritage of Britain'. With some new-found and very agreeable colleagues it proved a very enjoyable task, particularly in the seeking out of a mass of interesting pictures, both in colour and monochrome. I searched through my own collection, and brought out my painting of 'The Corridor' but the context of the book did not give any opportunity for using it. While working on the 'Heritage' book I met some other associates of the firm Michael Joseph who proved to be interested in the many other books of mine on railways that had been published, particularly as I had done a good deal of fact finding overseas. Before I had finished working on the Railway Heritage book I was getting involved, in the preliminary negotiating stages, for another one for one of their closely associated friends, Pelham Books, not with anything overseas as it turned out, but with the title 'Great British Trains' having the subtitle 'An evocation of a memorable age in travel'.

They asked for up to twenty illustrations in colour in addition to about one hundred black and white plates. I had many of the beautiful coloured postcards issued by the Locomotive Publishing Company, and these they swooped on. They had also acquired some modern photographs of trains in colour and then there were some paintings, of which I owned the copyright. Michael Joseph's office also had my own painting of the up 'Corridor' on Tebay troughs. This was produced and approved for the new book, and to accompany it I wrote a long chapter, because that train, both north and south of Carlisle, seemed a veritable flagship of a memorable age in travel. The script of that chapter, and the associated black and white pictures, covered the first introduction of the all-corridor train, tracing it through the building of the beautiful 12-wheeled bogie carriages, introduced in 1908. About the district in which I painted the picture which was reproduced in the Pelham book I wrote: 'The smooth, rounded summits of the fells that seem to encompass the railway on every side at Grayrigg are in striking contrast to the far-off Lakeland heights just glimpsed; but now the Corridor is quickening its pace again, as the line dips gently down into the Lune gorge, and begins a nearly-level five mile run to Tebay. The mountain solitude of this part of the line has now gone for ever, because the M6 motorway has been constructed higher up the slopes on the left hand side of the railway, and the trains themselves match, and surpass, the haste of the modern highway. Where the Corridor of old would have been running at 60 to 65 when it took water from the Dillicar troughs, the "Electric Scots" of today are often doing 100 m.p.h! Taking water at those troughs was a much photographed spectacle in the days of the London and North Western Railway, to record which brought some of the few moving-train camera experts from the South of England; but not for the Corridor, because it was not due to pass Tebay until 7.26 p.m. and by that time, even in summer, the gorge would be deep in the shadows of evening.'

In 1920, however, Mackay *did* photograph the down 'Corridor', not at Tebay but some 16 miles north, near Eden Valley Junction. Summer time had been introduced then, and astronomical midnight was not until 1 a.m. by Greenwich Mean Time. Moreover, due to wartime decelerations, the departure time of the train had been fixed at 1.15 p.m. instead of the traditional 2 p.m. Anyway Mackay was working on a clear cloudless evening, and on the high embankment of the gradual curve leading to the junction the train was in the setting sun throughout. As always with his work the photographic technique was immaculate, and I gathered he was very pleased with the result. But the train was taken almost broadside on, on that high embankment and showing nothing of the background scenery. Artistically, I am afraid I considered the picture a dead loss!

Chapter 8

Derwentwater, Friar's Crag

After my father's place of business had been moved from Reading to Barrow-in-Furness, in 1916, it was not long before I was browsing through the bookshops and the bookstall on the central Station there. In the war years the only coloured picture postcards that were for sale, seemingly, were of a series produced by Raphael Tuck & Sons for the Furness Railway. They were reproductions of paintings by A Heaton Cooper which had been published in some of the famous colourbook series by A & C Black. On each of these cards was printed the nearest station to the scene depicted. I have one showing the Raven Crag of Thirlmere having the imprint 'Ambleside Station', which latter was of course reached not by train but by one of the Furness Railway owned steam yachts plying on Windermere lake. This particular card is the only one now in my collection somewhat away from the regular activities of the Furness Railway though I believe Thirlmere was included in one of the coach tours that one could join at Ambleside. It was not until I went to London for my university studies that I found other coloured picture postcards featuring scenes in the Lake District.

A printer and publisher named J Salmon, working from Sevenoaks, Kent, was producing an extensive series of cards reproduced from paintings by A R Quinton of whom I had no previous knowledge. His subjects were nationwide, and I bought attractive pictures of the market cross at Salisbury, Whitby Abbey, and some delectable scenes in the South Downs, and the Thames Valley. Quinton's style of painting was not in the least impressionistic, very like the form that I had developed over the years, but I found some of the scenes he had depicted in the Lake District, particularly the country with which I was by that time familiar, by Grasmere, Rydal and Windermere a bit dull, by comparison to what he had painted elsewhere. They bore no resemblance to the vivid scenes in A Heaton Cooper's pictures as reproduced on the Furness Railway postcards. Then one day I was looking through a further selection of Quinton cards and with one of these I was pulled up short – Friar's Crag Derwentwater. This was one of the lakes we as a family had not yet visited. I bought the very attractive card, and looked forward to a future visit to the lake.

This was in 1922 or 3, and at that time our near-neighbours had built their new house on the vacant plot next to our own home. Those neighbours had a fine car in which my parents came to enjoy many trips to the Lake District in after years; but I was so intrigued by Quinton's painting of Friar's Crag Derwentwater that I made an enlarged copy of it, before I had ever seen the place itself! Comparing it with the postcard, after a lapse of nearly seventy years(!), it is evident that I added an extra hundred feet or so to the elevation of Cansey Pike just opposite across the lake to where the artist had taken his viewpoint. The water was calm, and I reproduced the drawing of a rowing boat in which a shirt-sleeved oarsman was giving his lady friend a ride around the lake. It was some years before my weekend Bank Holiday trips to my parents' home in Barrow coincided with an invitation from our next-door neighbour to make a trip out into the Lakes, and so for a time my painting of Friar's Crag remained as something out of my imagination.

For the whole of my time as a Graduate-Trainee at Westinghouse I was in 'digs' at various places in West London and I found solace at times in browsing through various bookshops in the West End. One day, in January 1927, I came across a series of fascinating little books with the generic title 'Things Seen...' The advertised twenty titles were mostly of regions far overseas, including China and Japan; but in the only four British ones I found 'Things seen in the English Lakes'. I swooped upon it. It was only a pocket-size volume, but of 150 pages, beautifully illustrated with fine photographs, and I took it home to my lodgings and literally devoured it. One of the pictures was of Friar's Crag, Derwentwater, which according to the inscription beneath was, according to John Ruskin, one of the four finest viewpoints in Europe. All the same remembering the coloured post-card from which I copied my painting of the scene I was surprised and disappointed that the artist Quinton had not included the beautiful trees which so effectively framed the scene in the photograph included in my new little book. I was in half a mind to alter my own painting, but for the fact that my father had had it framed, and that it was hanging on one of our walls in Barrow.

The author of that little book, W P Palmer, was the same as he who had written the magnificent book in the Black series first published some twenty years earlier, and illustrated with about seventy-five of A Heaton Cooper's superb water colours. In the 'Things Seen' he writes: 'Friar's Crag with its pines is so familiar in pictures that one views it critically as an old friend.' He goes on to tell that among the tree trunks there is a monument to John Ruskin, who claimed this view turned his mind for ever toward the glory of natural scene. He quotes him thus; 'The first time which I remember as an event in life was being taken by my nurse to the brow of Friar's Crag on Derwentwater. The intense joy, mingled with awe, that I had in looking through the mossy roots, over the crag, into the dark lake, has associated itself more or less with all twining roots of trees every since.' But an ancient dame of Keswick, who had heard much of this viewpoint, decided to brave her seventieth birthday by walking out to see for herself. She was not impressed! 'Ah think nowt of' yer Friar's Crag. There's nowt the-aw but wood and watter.' Books and quotations apart, however, I had not been to see for myself until the summer of 1927.

Then when I was at home for one of my Bank Holiday weekends the invitation came from our next-door neighbours, the Gilberts, to join them for a trip into the Lakes. My mother felt that it would be over-filling the car if she came, so my father and I went alone. Mrs Gilbert was a thorough-going North-Country woman steeped in all the lore of the countryside and I found her a delightful companion, while my father talked generalities and a little business with his host, sitting alongside the driver. We went via Windermere, Grasmere, Dunmail Raise and Thirlmere to Keswick, and then as I hoped turned south to the shores of Derwentwater. The main road towards Borrowdale is not adjacent to the lake itself beside Friar's Crag, but they stopped for me to get a near-distant view of it, and very beautiful it was. I saw it was very near to the foot of the lake, less than a mile from the centre of Keswick, and on subsequent visits to the Lakes I always make a point of walking out there, more appreciatively than the 'ancient dame' of seventy who walked out there on her birthday!

The main road reaches the lake side about half a mile south of Friar's Crag, but even then there was so much traffic as to make it, unfortunately, no place to linger sight-seeing. I should imagine that with road widening and other 'improvements' it must now be ten times worse. The Gilberts took us on to the head of the lake by Lodore. I had a postcard of one of the Quinton paintings of the Lodore Falls and I had not been very impressed. But from reading W P Palmer's little book I gather that the waterfall is one of moods dependent on the weather conditions. I saw it first in high summer, and appreciated what Palmer said about it. 'It is certainly worth a visit when the weather is moist. In drought it is a mere trickle between boulders, but in flood its voice is heard far down the dale and across the lake.' Another nineteenth-century lake poet, Robert Southey, described the cataract in its maximum intensity in such lyrical verse that most visitors coming to see it, especially in the summer, were grievously disappointed! On my first visit Mrs Gilbert took me instead to the head of the lake to enjoy the placid reed-strewn waters and the crags from which the waterfall sometimes dashes down in such furious spate. We picnicked near Lodore, before going farther than Borrowdale.

While relaxing over lunch I asked Mrs Gilbert if she had ever seen the Lodore Falls at their maximum intensity, but she said that when it was like that the main road beside the lake would be flooded – indeed as I had read in the little book 'Things seen in the English Lakes', after heavy rain one mighty lake extends ten miles from Grange Bridge, beyond the head of Derwentwater to Ouse Bridge at the end of Bassenthwaite lake. On this pleasant Bank Holiday week-end occasion we drove a little way farther south, passing the beautiful little hamlet of Grange-in-Borrowdale, where the mountains on either side close in to such dramatic effect that the location is well known as 'The Jaws of Borrowdale'. Just beyond this spectacular scene the Gilberts stopped for me to see The Bowder Stone.

It is a huge block of stone apparently resting on one corner. Tradition tells of its falling from the nearby crags, while another story attributes it, in age-old years, to the fall of a meteorite, I cannot quite credit the latter version, because if anything came from the sky, of such a size, it would make some considerable indentation in the ground, whereas The Bowder Stone rests on one edge. It is estimated to weigh about 1970 Tons!

Sometime after my first visit to Derwentwater and Borrowdale a hard spell of frost settled on the North Country, and the Gilberts invited my father and mother to join them on a trip to the Lakes to see the mountains in snow. On the chosen day the weather was gloriously fine, and the party left Barrow with high hearts. All went well until they had passed Ambleside, aiming to get near Keswick for lunch. But the lakeland roads were icy, and good driver though he was, Mr Gilbert skidded into the grass verge, and no manoeuvres could get him out. There was a telephone not very far away and Mrs Gilbert got out and began to feel her way. She had not gone far before she slipped and fell prostrate. She apparently could not get up, having bumped her head, and my father got out to go to the rescue. Having reached her he also slipped and fell on top of her! Gilbert exclaimed 'this is a tragedy' and he also got out, with no better result because himself fell before he reached the others, leaving my mother alone sitting in the car, with an ankle that could not be trusted on ice. How this adventure ended I cannot recall.

When my father retired at the end of 1930 the family home was moved from Barrow-in-Furness to Bushey, Herts, and because there it was no more than comfortable commuter travelling distance from my place of business I naturally went there to live. I was keen to keep up my visits to the North Country at Bank Holiday weekends, so I usually went alone, and indulged in walking over the areas where I had always been taken by car. These weekend trips from London gave further opportunities of studying the work of various locomotives on the way north, a study that was to bear rich fruit in after years, when I wrote countless articles about it in the technical press, and a few full-length books. In the early 1930s I usually made for Carlisle as a good jumping-off point for rambling activities in the Lake District. On one such weekend, I had taken the branch line

Derwentwater lake: Friar's Crag, looking across to Catbells.

train from Penrith and arrived in Keswick at teatime. The weather was gloriously fine, and after settling in to my digs I walked out to Friar's Crag. Although it was the eve of a Bank Holiday weekend there were few people about, and for half an hour I enjoyed the cosy pleasance of this much loved place.

Next morning I took the bus up to the furthest end of Borrowdale, to Rosthwaite, and then set out to climb the narrowing glen, and ultimately mountain track, to the summit of the Stye Head Pass, from which I looked down on Wastwater, and a distance glimpse of the Irish Sea. I had taken good care to take a substantial packed lunch with me, and I enjoyed the wild country and the clear mountain air to the full. I did not hurry down from these wild regions, but I was in Rosthwaite to have an outdoor tea in one of the cottages providing delicious alfresco meals. After this leisurely treat I was proposing to walk down Borrowdale, through the 'Jaws' to the head of Derwentwater, by Lodore, but I had hardly started on my way when I met an old friend from Giggleswick School, indeed the Second Master. When I first went there, in 1916, because of wartime conditions he had taken over the management of the junior boarding house for boys who were too young to go into the main hostel. I was in his care for four terms, and then as I climbed up the school I came under his guidance when sitting for the Oxford and Cambridge School Certificate, from which I passed into the Sixth Form. From my school days I remembered him as a classics scholar, possessor of a very pretty wit, and a fine cricketer, even though he was approaching middle age. It was great to see him again, and we gossiped for half an hour at the very least. After that weekend I did not see Friar's Crag for many years. I was getting married and my dear Olivia loved the country and we walked and rambled together. I had much business then in Scotland, and our pre-war holidays were mostly spent up there. Then came the war, and just afterwards Westinghouse gave us a brief respite of a single week's holiday. Our children were both at boarding school at the time so we dashed up to Ambleside, and stayed at one of the lakeside hotels. We did not travel far. We made one trip down the length of Windermere and took the train onwards to Furness Abbey as Olivia was interested to see the house which had been my home for so many years. We knocked at the house next door and found that the Gilberts were still in residence. She remembered me quite well, but he, in his old age, seemed to remember my father, but none of the rest of my family. The next visits to Barrow were all in my railway business, and it was not until Olivia and I were roving the country by private car that we came to visit the Lake District again. One of the first occasions, when we had planned a late-spring trip, was entrenched with a business appointment when I had to visit some important Westinghouse clients in Edinburgh, over some coal-mine mechanization with which I was very much involved. There were some evening occasions too, with ladies involved, so I took Olivia and a dear friend who was travelling with us – Eve Arrowsmith, elder sister of she who had consented to be our Trevor's Godmother some twenty years earlier. On our return south, there being no motorways built then, we planned to spend a night at Ambleside, and inevitably for me, I suppose, we detoured via Keswick, and made our way to the shores of Derwentwater – Once again we stood by Friar's Crag and took some photographs there.

Chapter 9
Clovelly – 'High Street'

Not long after I had gone to London to begin my university studies I was browsing in one of the stationer's shops in South Kensington and I came across a coloured postcard bearing a reproduction of one of A R Quinton's attractive water-colours. It was entitled 'High Street, Clovelly'. At that time I did not know, quite, where Clovelly was, but I bought the card and the next time I went home to Barrow I looked it up in the family atlas. I found it on the coast of North Devon, about half way between Bideford and Hartland Point. Apparently my mother had been there, long before she was married, on a coach tour from Ilfracombe, the coach being an open-topped charabanc drawn by two horses. She did not remember much about it, except that the passengers had to dismount at the top of the hill and walk down to the little harbour. She examined my postcard, and said 'High Street – I don't remember that there was any other street in the place.' And that was that. At that time I had not acquired any topographical books about Devonshire, and the card went into my personal archives at Barrow for the time being, to be brought out again in a later vacation when I though I would like to paint the scene in my own style.

Judging from descriptions of the place in each of the books I have bought subsequently I think that Quinton's painting on that postcard does not quite give an impression of the incredible steepness of the 'High Street'. I faithfully copied the basic outlines in my own picture, even to the extent of copying his drawings of the pannier-saddled donkeys that were employed in giving some visitors a lift up the street from the harbour to the place where the charabancs were parked on the level ground at the top of the hill. I also included the white-bearded old gaffer who was tending one of the donkeys. The cottages and their gaily-painted open windows were meat and drink to my brush, so also were the flowers and climbing shrubs alongside, with one exception. In the right-hand lower side of this painting the artist included a russet-leaved tree that even now I have failed to recognize. I wonder if the painting was made in the autumn, but even then trees of that shape do not usually assume their autumn colours uniformly. Anyway, I started to copy it. My mother and sister went out for the afternoon and left me at work. Never shall I forget that day! I struggled with that tree, and when they came back and it was time to clear me away and lay for nursery tea, I had more or less given up the job in disgust. Next day I washed out all my previous efforts and started with a clean piece of paper in that corner of the drawing paper. Eventually I got it to my satisfaction but always looked at the picture, still hanging on the wall of my present home, and remember the struggle I had with that climbing tree!

Some little time after I had painted that picture I began collecting books about Devonshire. The first was Lady Northcote's magnificient *Devon – its Moorlands, Streams and Coasts.* Then came Baring Gould's *A Book of Dartmoor,* followed by V C Clinton-Baddeley's *Devon,* in the post-war series of Black's Colour Books. Also from my father's library there was always A H Norway's *Highways and Byways in Devon and Cornwall* to refer to. As far as Clovelly was concerned my immediate references to three of the above mentioned books were, I must admit, at first only to the illustrations. I should explain I had got myself so steeped in the scenery and railways of the southern coastal stretch from Exeter to Totnes and Dartmouth, and the wonderful opportunities for photographing that they provided, that I came to revel, long after those joyous holidays, in the history, folklore and all else of the region I had so enjoyed. The books, no less than the photographs I had amassed, sustained me during many hours in London digs. As for Clovelly, I found the pictures in the books I had collected generally far from satisfying, that is, I hasten to add, as was in any way a compliment to Quinton's painting of the 'High Street'.

The artist in Lady Northcote's book, F J Widgerey, was a Devonshire man and he provided a gallery of superb pictures. With Clovelly however he produced an almost bird's-eye view from the top of the escarpment from some distance east of the village, and while the picture was charming in itself it conveyed not a clue as to what was hidden among the trees below. Clinton-Baddeley's book in the lovely series published by A & C Black was illustrated by Sutton Palmer whose work I had greatly admired in various of the sumptuous volumes in the earlier larger format series published before the fateful year 1914, which were then in my father's library. In turning to the North Devon pages of the newly-published book I was not disappointed though even here the artist had not pictured the 'High Street' as rendered by Quinton. Sutton Palmer painted the high-level view, as Widgerey had done but from nearer at hand, but he had also a scene on the beach, at low tide, including the jetty, but not revealing the topsy-turvy array of cottages that straggled up the very steep hillside. The artist in Norway's *Highways and Byways in Devon and Cornwall* eschewed entirely the task of committing the village itself to pen and pencil. He merely drew a picture called 'The Gateway', and that was that.

It was not until the middle of World War II that I actually made my first personal visit to North Devon. Then blessed with an exiguous week's leave Olivia and I took our young family to Combe Martin. There was no opportunity of touring around then. We went by train to Ilfracombe and because of wartime restrictions of service we could not go the direct GWR route from Taunton to Barnstaple and had to go via Exeter and the Southern Railway. I read up Lady Northcote's book and enjoyed the beautiful pictures, covering the coast from Barnstaple through to Ilfracombe, but nothing as yet about Clovelly. The opportunity came many years later, when Olivia and I had made a habit of making an early summer motoring tour, for a week, and taking our dear friend Eve Arrowsmith with us. This trip, believe it or not began at the Shakespeare Memorial Theatre, Stratford-on-Avon: on the morning afterwards we drove to Beaulieu in the New Forest and thereafter made our way, by easy stages, to Penzance. Our next port of call was Bude, where we were well placed for a visit to Clovelly the following day. In anticipation of this I had read up the descriptions of the place in my three books.

I have very often found that descriptions of places of great beauty are sometimes disappointing in that the author in question allows himself, or herself, to be carried away to the heights of extravagance that an ordinary reader finds tiresome, or on the other hand to belittle the beauty of the place as something that is rather overrated. Both my long-lived parents were dead by the time of which I am now writing and all the choicest books in my father's library had been added to my own collection, including some two dozen of the 'Highways and Byways' series. Before we set out on this particular trip I got out Norway's book on 'Devon and Cornwall'. It was published in 1897, and I take the liberty of quoting him, thus:

'What is like Clovelly, and with that similitude shall I make clear the aspect of the most exquisite town in England? There is none. One is the richer in experience for having seen Clovelly; elsewhere there is nothing like it. I sit on the balcony of the New Inn, a pleasant hostelry with old bow windows. I have but this moment left the woods, and their green shade is close to my right hand. Below me lies a scene more exquisite than could have been devised by the wit of man deliberately set to produce what is picturesque. For it is surely very strange that this village, during all the centuries of its existence, has grown, if grown it really has, along lines of perfect beauty. How many villages one has seen defaced and ruined by the destruction of an old house front, or the building of new shops? But here is nothing, absolutely nothing, commonplace or ugly; not a modern house front, not a shop save here and there a cottage window filled with photographs or gaudy Barum ware. Not even a dissenting chapel breaks the perfect curve with which the narrow street drops down the hillside between high peaked and gabled houses and humbler slated cottages with deep bow windows and diamond panes, and the fresh red-brown Virginia creeper trailing over them. The street is cut in steps and paved with cobbles, and up it comes a string of donkeys limping from the quay, straying into the cool shade of every open doorway which they pass, while the women come out and hang over the green balconies above and scold and chatter at the luckless driver, who defends himself in his slow western speech, and at last with many thwackings sets the head of the poor patient donkey straight again, and goes up three steps more when the same process

Clovelly, the street, based on a picture-postcard by A R Quinton.

is repeated. It is warm and sunny. The white clouds drift slowly over
the tree tops. A little way below me the street makes a bend, and over
the houses I see the bay, blue and brown and dotted with fishing
boats; and across it lie the golden sands of Braunton and the dim
high ground which stand round Ilfracombe.'

Lady Northcote, whose book was published a quarter century after
Mr Norway's, writes 'Eleven miles west of Bideford is Clovelly. Here
one feels, rather despairingly, that anyone who has seen this wonderful village can listen to no description of it; while to those who
have never seen it, no description is of any value.' She then proceeds
to dodge the issue by quoting lyrical descriptions of it by Charles
Kingsley and Charles Dickens. Her own concluding comment is that:
'The harbour is very small, but on a cliff-bound dangerous coast it is
one of the very few between Bideford and Padstow. Clovelly's great
herring fishery used to be famous, but it is not now so large as it used
to be.' So to Clinton-Baddeley. Soon after the end of World War I the
publishers A & C Black, with whom I myself had some pleasant and
profitable associations forty years further on, began to add to the
sumptuously produced 'Colour Books', of which my father had been
a keen collector. In the post-war world, however, they would have
been too expensive and so a much cheaper version was introduced, a
new edition embodying all the original text but only 24 colour
plates, instead of the 60 or 70 in the pre-war versions. I cannot trace
that there was a book on 'Devon' in the original series, and I believe
that Clinton-Baddeley's work was a new addition to the series.

He writes 'The first time I saw Clovelly I realized at once that it is
exactly like its photographs, but that nevertheless I had entirely
misconceived it. A picture may portray a special scene with accuracy,
but it cannot include its setting; and at Clovelly the setting is of
paramount importance. Everyone is familiar with the picture of the
little paved street – so steep that the chimneys of one house are level
with the bedrooms of the next, so narrow that each cottage peers
into the windows of the house across the way. Everyone knows the
gay tiny gardens, fragrant with jessamine and honeysuckle, decked
with geraniums and fuchsias; and the donkeys, and the sleighs, and
the steps; and how the street corkscrews to the sea. But you will never
realize from a picture that round the corner on the right, at the top

of the little street, the paved way still mounts upwards; and that, when you do reach the road, you are still more than three hundred feet below the highway at Clovelly Dykes – a British camp, seven hundred feet above the sea. Clovelly is sunk more deep beneath the hills, and hidden more cunningly among the woods, than ever a picture can tell. The charabancs have found it out, of course, and the street is full of caterers; but despite the stream of visitors that come there in the summer, Clovelly is still cut off from the world. I feel that particularly. The houses and the people of Clovelly are in no wise degraded to the state of exhibits in a World museum, like the old cities of Italy. They are leading a purposeful life. If you like to go and see them doing it, you, and the commerce you bring with you, are kindly welcome; but they are not acting a play for your benefit; the sleighs and the donkeys are not stage properties, nor are the fairy-like gardens so much scenery. I think Clovelly is almost the only famous place I ever saw which has not been over-praised. It is narrower, steeper, higher, older, than ever I pictured it. It has been rebuilt, of course, but it has not suffered therefrom; for the new houses have followed old designs, without in the least masquerading as antiques – witness the candid dates upon their foreheads.

'Walking down Clovelly street is much harder than walking up it; but you must go down, for at the bottom is the fish market, and the pier, and from the pier a wonderful view of the village. Here the cliffs are grandly tall, and they have lost their grimness. They are not jagged or menacing, but broad and solid, the whole magnificently clothed in trees, and festooned with luxuriant vegetation. See Clovelly now, scrambling up the cliff among the trees!'

It was a beautiful day in early summer when we came to Clovelly. We parked our car at the top of the cliff, and then made our way down 'The Street'. Olivia and Eve had not read any descriptions previously, and they were overwhelmingly entranced. So was I, taking many photographs on our way down to the harbour, where we sat on the jetty for some time. Now, forward another thirty years, to almost a complete century after Arthur H Norway wrote his book. By this time I was already into the higher-eighties of my own life-span, and because of certain disabilities having to have a resident nurse in the house, from time to time. In 1992 one of the splendid young women which the British Nursing Association sent to minister to my needs was a truly lovely girl, born in Rhodesia, of European parentage, who had done her early training in South Africa but was at the moment in England to gain further experience. In between turns of duty she had been touring round the UK and had been to Clovelly. Seeing the picture on one of my walls she gathered that I was interested, but she said she was afraid I would be disappointed to see it now, it was so commercial. From what other friends of mine, Australians this time, found when they attempted to see certain beauty spots in Cornwall I fear that Clovelly has gone the same way. So, my painting remains as a 'period price'.

Chapter 10

In 1924: the Up Postal Train leaving Penzance

In 1924 the annual month's holiday for our family was to be at Penzance. While I had graduated as a B.Sc. in Engineering earlier that year my father had decided to give me an extra post-graduate year, and so I enjoyed yet another three months of vacation before going back to college in October, and I could, for the last time, spend the whole four weeks of their holiday with the family. I took my bicycle of course, and on the very next morning after arrival in Penzance I rode off towards Marazion to seek out some places for railway photography. I had a walking permit covering the whole line from Penzance to east of Truro, but the line farthest west in Cornwall was not very pretty scenically, and I turned back to explore the running sheds at Ponsandane. The foreman made me very welcome but I found to my disappointment that the engines on shed were almost exclusively of the very efficient, outside-cylindered, Churchward 'Mogul' type; excellent for the job in Cornwall, but with the sameness about them that did not appeal to a photographer once he had taken one or two of them. They were also in the plain green, unlined livery of wartime.

I walked around the yard taking pictures of several of them, in various stages of preparation for main line passenger duties. After the Cornish Riviera Express, which then left at 10 a.m., there were expresses to Liverpool and Manchester, to Birmingham and Wolverhampton, and a second London train which took the through coaches for Aberdeen which had been introduced in 1921. The shed foreman delighted in telling me how useful, efficient and economical the 2-6-0s were for all these duties, and almost casually he added that there was a very pretty engine at the back of the shed. Would I like to see it? And there, in the darkest recesses of the building, completely unphotographable, was an express passenger 4-6-0 of the 'Saint' class, not quite in perfect external condition, but looking very colourful compared to the work-a-day 'Moguls' outside in the yard. I noticed that the 4-6-0 was stationed at Exeter, and the foreman told me that Exeter men brought the West of England Postal special through, and lodged the day in Penzance before taking the eastbound Postal back at 6 p.m. I was told that the one engine worked the train right through to Paddington, via Bristol, with a second Exeter crew relieving those who had worked up from Penzance. This second set lodged in London on arrival, and brought the same engine back. It was only on arrival at Exeter on the down journey that there was a change of engines.

At this distance in time I cannot remember the name of the engine so secreted in the shed at Ponsondane; I believe it may have been *Saint Bernard*. But if it was I did not see it again during all the time we stayed in Penzance. A train departure at 6 p.m. was about as inconvenient as possible as far as family arrangements were concerned. Wherever we might be staying, nursery tea at 5 p.m. was a deadline date so far as my mother's arrangements were concerned. We had private apartments, and the landladies whether they were in Penzance, Inverness, or anywhere else had to confirm, or else – ! 'Tea' was always the nursery variety; never in my bachelor days at home having 'high tea'. It was always thickly cut bread, liberally spread with butter and home-made jam. Not until we had imbibed two, or even three slices of this were we offered any cake. To get to the station to photograph the up Postal leaving at 6 p.m. involved bolting my bread, butter and jam, dispensing with cake altogether, and pedalling my way to the railway for dear life. It was a 6 or 7 minutes run from our lodgings, and then I had to park the bicycle, and go through the formalities of getting on to the line. I found the light had been favourable in the morning when I photographed the procession of expresses leaving from 10 a.m., but was far otherwise in the early evening, with the line beneath a high retaining wall on the landward side masking what light there was from the setting sun.

My first 'shot' involved a 'Star' class four-cylinder 4-6-0 and this was not very successful. From later explorations I found that there was a much more convenient access to the railway, beyond the high wall that flanked the main road. It had the advantage of avoiding the need of going through the station buildings, parking my bicycle, and submitting to the formalities of showing my walking pass. By this means I could get farther down the line and a clear view of the left-hand side of the train in clear, albeit somewhat slanting, sunshine. One evening I got a satisfactory picture of the 'Saint' class engine *Clevedon Court* leaving, with a fine exhaust plume. It has been used in one or two of my books and articles. Still continuing to seek out more advantageous position, in between times, I walked along the length of that retaining wall, and found that it gave a very pleasant view over the harbour, as a background to the railway. There were then four tracks at this point, the main down and up running lines into the station, and a lengthy siding each side of these latter. This was where I should go for my next shot at the Postal coming out.

But when I was at the shed a few days later I saw that the 'Saint' class engine *Lady of Lynn* had come in overnight from Exeter. She did not look anything like so 'pretty' as the previous 4-6-0s I had seen, because she had fairly recently been repainted in the plain, unlined green of wartime. Moreover she had been fitted with one of the plain tapered chimneys that were being used on the later 'Moguls' and also on the new 'Abbey' series of four-cylinder 4-6-0 express passenger engines. As a wartime expedient they were admirable but they destroyed the majestic look of the pre-war engines with their massively built chimneys adorned with broad copper tops. I decided to photograph *Lady of Lynn* coming out of Penzance that evening from rail level, almost head-on. I did not see her again during that holiday, but more than four years later when I was going to Barrow for the Easter weekend, and decided to travel up from Paddington to Shrewsbury and then cut across to Crewe. The 2.10 p.m. train was running in two portions and the relief, leaving at 2.05, was hauled by *Lady of Lynn*, going right through to Shrewsbury. I joined the train

On the GWR in 1924, the up Postal Train leaving Penzance hauled by the delightfully named engine Lady of Shalott.

and was rewarded with some of the most brilliant running I have ever had on that route.

Reverting to my first stay in Penzance in due course I found the delightfully named engine *Lady of Shalott* on the Postal job. But when I went to my retaining wall position to photograph her coming out on the evening and all-night run to Paddington, I found that a rake of rather scruffy coaches had been parked in the siding next to the sea-shore. This rather spoiled the picturesque background that I hoped to get, for the *Lady of Shalott* was beautiful turned out in full post-war Great Western glory. But it was a cloudy evening, and what with the disappointing background the result was not one of my more glamorous railway photographs, though the documentation was clear enough, as will be told later. The *Lady of Shalott* made no other visits to Penzance on the Postal train when I was there, but then on our return home by the Cornish Riviera express to Paddington, while we had the usual 'Mogul' from the start, at Truro the *Lady of Shalott* took over and I was able to log an interesting example of her running between Truro and Plymouth. Those were the days before the Cornish Riviera Express carried a through coach for Newquay, and so there was no stop at Par. The 54¾ miles between Truro and Plymouth were run non-stop in 79¼ minutes, an average of 41½ m.p.h. and bringing us in nearly 2 minutes early.

This memory of the *Lady of Shalott*, and the photograph I had taken of her leaving Penzance on the up Postal, then lay in my archives for more than twenty years, and then the picture was taken out in rather unusual circumstances. Towards the end of the Second World War, George Lake, the founder editor of the new monthly magazine, *Railways*, with which I had been associated almost from its inception, was branching out into book publication and he asked me if I would undertake to write a book on locomotive working. He sent me copies of two volumes he had already published, both by authors well known in their respective fields of interest and I was impressed by the scholarship of the writing and of the excellence of production, albeit strictly conforming to the restrictions of the day. My own, published in 1947, worked out as a 250-page job, with numerous diagrams, many photographs and a dust jacket drawn by one of Lake's publisher friends, which I liked very much but which earned the criticism of one chap who thought the draughtmanship was poor, and he could have done it better himself! But George Lake also wanted a colour plate, and having been to our house occasionally and seen my work he asked me to do one specially.

The second chapter in my book was titled 'Some great runs with "Saints" and "Stars"', and on reflection I thought of the shot of the Postal leaving Penzance that I hoped to get, but was balked by that array of old carriages. I got the photograph out again and started to sketch. I had been to Penzance just at the time when Sir Felix Pole, as General Manager of the GWR, was engaged in smartening up the whole railway after the depressing war years, and another move was to restore the 'chocolate and cream' livery of the entire carriage stock. This was inevitably a gradual process. This livery had been abandoned in the early 1900s and restoration began on the sets of coaches for the principal expresses. Any extras were often painted in the crimson lake style, as was the leading coach of the up Cornish Riviera when I photographed it near Marazion on the very first morning we were at Penzance. Some of the vehicles on the Postal train as I saw it in 1924 were in the old livery, but when I painted the whole train in 'chocolate and cream'. Apparently I dated the picture 1946. It was nicely reproduced, though the book itself did not have a very gratifying sale.

I did not set eyes upon the train for more than thirty years since that holiday in Penzance, and it was only when I began to go to London on business and occasionally to stay for an evening meeting of one of the technical institutions with which I was professionally associated that I saw the train, always of course after dark. The westbound Postal train left Paddington at that time at 10.10 p.m. My own return train to Bath was the 9.50 p.m. Penzance 'sleeper'. This was a long and heavy train and did much intermediate business. It had a leisurely running schedule and made lengthy station stops. The Postal on the other hand was sharper timed, up to the standard of the two-hour Bristol expresses. It also did a lot of intermediate business, not by station stops but by use of the apparatus which collected and delivered mails at full speed by means of the traductor gear fitted to several of the special mail vans. The Penzance 'sleeper' was put on to the relief line while making its passenger stop at

Didcot. The Postal was booked non-stop from Reading to Bath, and always when I was travelling down from London I used to look out and see it come flying through. Although not so heavy a train as our own it needed first-class locomotive work and the speed on level track was usually nearly 70 m.p.h. through Didcot.

I had found that the engine working and the manning arrangements had been completely changed since I photographed the train on that faraway holiday in Penzance. The westbound train, which I saw frequently, at any rate between Paddington and Bristol formed part of the duties of the Bristol 'mileage link', an arrangement which put the senior drivers at Bath Road shed then into one large link, which involved, on regular occasions their working express passenger trains to London, Salisbury, Weymouth, Newton Abbot, Cardiff, Shrewsbury and Wolverhampton. The westbound Postal was a return working from London from running the evening business express from Bristol to Paddington. The 'Mileage Link' at Bristol did not include any 'double-home' turns – the railway term for a long duty that involved lodging away overnight, as was the case with the Exeter men working the Postal through to Penzance when I saw the train frequently in 1924.

When thirty years later the boffins at British Railways headquarters set out to alter this all hell was let loose in Bristol. The 'mileage' men at Bath Road shed, *en bloc*, went out on strike, and some of the other Western Region sheds, like Old Oak Common and Newton Abbot, were sympathetic, with many of the top-link enginemen abstaining from duty. This trouble could not have come at a worse time for me personally, for I was deeply involved professionally with the International Railway Congress Association meetings which were being held in Great Britain that year. Fortunately the men at Swindon were working normally and I had to hire taxis from Bath to catch South Wales trains that stopped there. I cannot recall how this dispute was settled, but fortunately it did not last for long, and the offending duties, which I understood involved quite minor trains, were discreetly withdrawn. So far as the Postal train was concerned, its timings were not published in the public timetables; but my friends at Paddington at that time sent me copies of the workings, so I was able to see, and appreciate, the fast schedule worked by the 10.10 p.m. for Paddington.

Around 1955 there were one or two survivors of the 'Star' class 4-6-0s stationed at Bath road shed that had undergone heavy repairs and had been turned out looking very smart. I saw one of these, the *Princess Margaret* on the 5.15 p.m. from Bristol to Paddington, which meant that she would come back on the Postal. This was too good a chance to miss and so I wrote to the Motive Power superintendent asking if I could be granted a footplate pass for the round trip. I was aware that certain restrictions were imposed on the working of postal trains generally from my experience in writing up 'Scottish Night Mails of the LMS' for *The Railway Magazine*. But no difficulty was met on the West of England Postal train and permission to ride was readily forthcoming. The engine this time was the *Malmesbury Abbey*, one of the twelve units of the class built at Swindon just after the end of the First World War, and at first finished in the drab austerity livery of wartime, with a plain, tapered, cast-iron chimney like the one I photographed on *Lady of Lynn* in 1924. But the 'Abbeys' were soon decked in all the pre-war glory of Great Western express locomotives, and when I rode *Malmesbury Abbey* that night she looked a picture.

A minor temporary difficulty faced me just before the trip. In the two-hour break in Paddington between our arrival from Bristol and departure of the postal I had left my enginemen friends to get a snack supper. The Postal train left from one of the 'closed' platforms in the station, and I came up against a huge railway policeman when I attempted to enter. A travelling ticket cut no ice with him, and even my footplate pass was regarded with some suspicion; but fortunately the locomotive inspector who had been with us from Bristol came up and explained matters, and all was well. We had a grand run that night. Because of some early delays we had left Reading about five minutes late, but then, with a clear road we ran the 71 miles to Bath in 69½ minutes, and arrived just one minute early, having achieved a maximum speed of 82 m.p.h. down the Dauntsey bank. It was a memorable reminder of my earlier contacts with the West of England Postal special.

Chapter 11
Grasmere – the Island, looking towards Dunmail Raise

I should imagine that it was no more than a coincidence that I should have been born in January 1905 in a little house named 'Grasmere', in the Warwickshire village, as it was then, of Sutton Coldfield. And even more of a coincidence that I should have been given the same name as that of the patron saint of the little church in the lakeland village of Grasmere, Oswald. There is a family story about this latter. Neither of my mother's brother or sister had any boys, and she was anxious to keep the family name of Stevens intact so she gave me the Christian name of Stevens, and 'Stevie' became my family name still being used by some of my oldest friends. Christian names were not often used in my public school days, and it was not until I got to London and joined Toc H that Ossie, as the obvious abbreviation of Oswald, became the name that I was best known by.

By that time I had become well and truly immersed in the fascinating lore of the Lake District, whether it was breathtaking scenery, the physical and geographical reasons for the lie of the land, or the way the Furness Railway provided for the enjoyment of that glorious country. When I left Giggleswick School at the end of the summer term of 1921 we had not journeyed beyond the head of Windermere, in our journeys from the Lakeside Branch of the Furness Railway, though the family had been to Coniston, and while staying at Seascale we hired a wagonette to take us to see Wastwater. With my father's wholehearted approval however I began collecting postcards, coloured and otherwise, of the Lakeland country, and at one time there was keen competition between my sister and me as to who could assemble the most attractive collection. One of the most useful sources of supply, for me at any rate, was the bookstall on Barrow Central station, where I was permitted to go on frequent occasions.

There was a method in this particular ploy, because the bookstall there always had a large collection of the picture postcards issued by the Furness Railway itself. None of the pre-grouping railway companies of Great Britain had developed the publicity sense to a greater extent than the Furness, not even the Great Western! When my good friends the publishers A & C Black brought out their beautiful book on the English Lakes, with seventy or so coloured plates by the superb Lakeland artist A Heaton Cooper, in 1905, the Furness Railway got in on the publicity act, and with the assistance of the publishers Rapheal Tuck and Sons arranged to reproduce many of the pictures in that book 'in glorious technicolour' as the modern saying goes. The postcards were superbly reproduced, indeed those that I still have are just as good as the pictures in the original book, of which I have got a first edition. The postcards are also collectors pieces in another respect. On the backs there is a fine reproduction, not in colour this time, of the Furness Railway coat of arms, and on the left hand side a note that 'The Furness Railway passes through the English Lake District, and along some of the picturesque Coastal Scenery in the Kingdom.' Another reminder of the times lay in the note within the space for the postage stamp 'Inland ½d; Foreign 1d'!!

My father had not yet begun collecting the beautiful first editions of the famous Black Colour Books so that the Furness Railway picture postcard reproductions were the only means I had of seeing the beauties of the district. But my sister and I avidly collected copies of the equally famous monochrome photographs published by Abrahams, of Keswick, and I began to learn what the country north of the Waterhead Pier, Ambleside, was like. This was the furthest we could go on our afternoon trips from our home, near Furness Abbey, by train to Windermere Lake Side station, and then the whole length of the Lake by steam yacht. The bookstall at Lake Side station also had some attractive cards, also published by the Furness Railway, of the various yachts that plied on the lake. These were magnificently produced photographs, and I have all these in my possession to this day. The subjects also included the one yacht then sailing on Coniston Lake, the *Lady of the Lake*, and also the gondola, but we never managed a trip on either of these.

I have been a long time coming to Grasmere itself, indeed it was not until we had been living in Barrow for seven years that we ventured north of Waterhead, Ambleside. Then it was in the course of my long, summer, university vacation holidays when I returned home from London at the beginning of July. My sister was still at school at the time, and in the usually fine and settled weather which we enjoyed that year, I believe it was 1923, my mother and I made several trips to the lakes. We took the bus from Ambleside to Grasmere, we visited Coniston, hopefully for a trip on the Gondola (which did not arrive until we had left the lakeside to catch our train back home!) and of course paid a visit to the Ravenglass and Eskdale Railway. On that first visit I was not impressed with Grasmere. The weather was hot and sultry, and there was not much colour in the landscape. Then our travelling arrangements from Barrow began to change. When we moved from Reading there was a vacant plot immediately adjacent to our new house, in Croslands Park, on the very outermost fringe of the residential part of the town, so much so that when we were travelling anywhere by train we used Furness Abbey station, except when going by the very few trains that did not stop there. Soon after the war one of my father's business friends bought the plot and had a fine house built thereon.

He was a jeweller and came originally from the Black Country, but his wife was a Lancastrian with all the most innate love of the North Country. They became the closest friends my parents ever formed when they lived in Barrow, and as he was a keen and experienced motorist they had many trips out into the Lake District which she knew and loved. The family friendship was not fully consummated by the time my university spell was ending and I was joining Westinghouse, and instead of several months holiday in the summer not to mention good spells at Christmas and Easter, I had to be content with no more than a fortnight in one year. Fortunately at bank holiday weekends, as at Easter and Whitsun, the London office where I was based remained closed until the Wednesday morning, and taking advantage of the cheap fares that then prevailed on the

British Railways at weekends I usually went up to Barrow, and was usually invited to join our next-door neighbours on some motoring expedition into the Lake District. Needless to say I always had my camera with me, and with Mr Gilbert's guidance managed to obtain some choice photographs.

Despite the disappointment I felt after my first visit to Grasmere I had one of the Abraham photographs of the Lake, and one Sunday morning in my top floor room overlooking Queens Gate Gardens in South Kensington I roughed up a water-colour sketch of the little island in the middle of the lake. I finished it on the next time I went to Barrow, duly scrutinized and approved by Mrs Gilbert. On a later visit they took me to some equally delightful spots around Grasmere Lake. In January 1927, nearly a year after I had painted my picture, I bought a charming little book entitled *Things Seen on the English Lakes*. It was by the same author W P Palmer who had written the fabulous colour book published by A & C Black in 1905, which by that time was in my father's library. I was very amused by his reference to Grasmere as 'a haunt of men and women, not of poets and philosopher alone. Few artists have caught the wandering spirit of this vale. The reflections and living shades on the lake baffle brush and pen alike.' These thoughts about Grasmere must not be taken lightly. Palmer was not a mere journalist who wrote nice things about the Lake District. He was a dalesman born and bred, though always proud of his first seeing the light of day south of the Dunmail Raise! For many years he was editor of *The Fell and Rock Journal*.

I had finished my water-colour of Grasmere lake some months before I bought his book *Things Seen in the English Lakes*, and at first I was more concerned with the numerous fine photographs than with the letter press. In his earlier book, published by Black's in 1905, out of more than seventy lovely colour plates there was only one of Grasmere lake, a high-level view from Loughrigg Terrace looking north, with the lake itself a mere pool backed by the knobbly mass of Helm Crag behind the village and the heights of Seat Sandal towering above Dunmail Raise to the east. Our neighbour, Mrs Gilbert, had seen the original painting from which this picture was reproduced, and she was quite scathing in her comments. In the foreground of his picture the artist A Heaton Cooper had put a

Grasmere, the island, looking north to Helm Crag and Seat Sandal.

group of foxgloves in all their beauty. So, she averred, foxgloves could never grow in that location; and she was a good naturalist. On one of my weekend visits they took me to the viewpoint on Loughrigg Terrace and showed me why foxgloves could not possibly grow there!

W P Palmer christened the deep glen in which the little river Rothay flows out of Grasmere lake into Rydal Water and thence to the head of Windermere as 'Wordsworthshire'. Certainly the district included the two houses, Dove Cottage and Rydal Mount, where the poet did most of his work, and Palmer in his two books makes little attempt to disguise the fact that he, who had lived his whole life exploring and rambling through every nook and cranny and every high pass and every summit however inaccessible, considered 'Wordsworthshire' his favourite region. To revert to Grasmere itself, after my father had retired from the bank in Barrow, and my parents had come to live near London, within commuter distance of my place of business we had a visit from a North Country friend. The water-colour I had painted of Grasmere was then framed in a place of honour on the staircase leading from the entrance hall. Climbing the stairs in a tour of inspection of our new property she stopped short, saying: 'That's Grasmere is it not?' The house inspection was then interrupted for at least a quarter of an hour while she dilated on the beauties of the light, colour and reflections that I had some-how got into the picture. My own thoughts were very far from the Lake District at the time, and when our visitor had gone I had not time to look up either of Palmer's books. It was not until many years later that I found his assertion that 'the reflections and living shades on the lake baffle brush and pen alike'. I mentally commented: 'not bad, Ossie Nock!'

In the Black's colour book of 1905 there was certainly a beautiful picture of the little village church of Grasmere, dedicated to St Oswald, but it was many more years before I learned the story of the eminent man whose name was bequeathed by my father on me. The year was then 1940 and at that time we were far away from the family house in Bushey where my picture of Grasmere still, I believe, hung on the staircase wall. I had then been married for more than three years and on the outbreak of war in 1939 the engineering staff of Westinghouse had been moved from the Company headquarters in

London, Kings Cross, to Chippenham. By the late summer of 1940 Hitler's armies had overrun the Allied forces on the Western Front, the British Expeditionary Force had been evacuated from Dunkirk, and the aerial 'Battle of Britain' was still in full blast. Holidays of the usual length were out of the question, but to give the staff some respite, before what promised to be a pretty grim winter the Westinghouse management gave all the staff a weekend's long leave at the end of August. My mother and sister were staying with us at Chippenham at the time, so Olivia and I decided to go up to the Lake District. At such short notice we could hardly expect to get accommodation in Ambleside, but we fixed upon Kendal, from which plenty of public transport was then available.

How we got there I do not recall, but once at Waterhead it seemed that wartime restrictions were non-existent. The lake seemed positively *en fête* with yachts and pleasure craft of all descriptions and the shores thronged with other holidaymakers. Jill, our two-year-old daughter, enjoyed it enormously, but I am afraid Olivia and I had thoughts that were straying elsewhere! But I have still got one priceless souvenir from that brief holiday. While in Kendal I visited a bookshop in the main street of the town and bought a copy of one of the later Black's colour books *Wild Lakeland*. It was one of the inter-war series, much cheaper than the sumptuous volumes issued before 1914, with 24 coloured plates instead of the 70 or so in the earlier productions. *Wild Lakeland* was written by a Scotsman named MacKenzie MacBride, but the colourplates were a joy to behold, all by the same artist as those of the earlier Black book, A Heaton Cooper. In my then prevailing mood I did little more than feast my eyes on the marvellously evocative paintings of lakeland scenery contained in that lovely book. It was not until some time later that I began to read the author's vivid descriptions and his poetry. For Mackenzie MacBride was also a long resident in Lakeland, and his script continues to provide me with much enjoyable reading, even including the passage headed 'Grasmere's Saint who resembled the Kaiser'!

MacBride's first chapter in his book was entitled 'Lakeland under Water', and in his first pages there was more than an echo of my own picture of Grasmere, which I had painted from memory, not from nature. I take leave to quote from the pages of that book: 'To me,' he writes, 'when the skies are clear and no mists float over the noble hills that stretch across from Helvellyn and Fairfield to the Scawfell group, they have lost their greatest charm. They do not attract so much. Why is this?' On the next page he continues: 'The most subtle of all our sensations, the most lovely of all our poems, the most captivating of all our pictures are those which bring us up against the great shadow – the unknown perhaps the unknowable, who can say!' And finally 'The scenery that gives us this great sense of mystery, of the gigantic, the unseen, the unknown, is nowhere if it is not here when Lakeland is under water. Then the rain fills burn and beck with glittering splendour and there arises a subtle and lovely murmur of the smooth-going Rothay or Derwent . . .'

Then he has another chapter, No. 18 in the book, entitled 'Grasmere of the Gardens'. He opens this chapter with a poem of his own, twelve idyllic verses beginning 'I know a garden, free and fair . . .', but in a couple of pages he comes to Grasmere's saint, Oswald, who he thinks had traits in his nature more akin to those of the ex-Emperor of Germany than a man who had learned his Christianity in Iona! MacBride's book was published first in 1922, when memories of the First World War were vividly around us. When I bought his book at Kendal in 1940, in the midst of another German war, our sentiments, such as they were, were directed towards a far more evil, wicked personality than ever 'Kaiser Bill' was in earlier days. St Oswald on the other hand had far more of the crusading spirit than either of the German 'führers'. He had been taught Christianity, and embraced his new religion with such fervour that when he had been restored to his father's throne in Northumbria he set out on a crusade against the Welsh and lost his own life in battle.

Lastly I turn again to W P Palmer and his references to 'Wordsworthshire', for in the little village church of St Oswald at Grasmere there are interned not only the Poet Laureate himself, but his wife and his sister Dorothy, whose authorship also adorns English literature.

Chapter 12

The paddle-steamer 'Waverley' navigating stern-first from the pier at Lochgoilhead

It used to be the fashion with less elegant and less knowledgeable travel writers to term any busy junction or concentration of traffic as the 'Charing Cross' of such a district. Why Charing Cross I found it a little hard to imagine, because that area of the West End of London, although busy enough in itself, was, and is still not, a major traffic centre. Even so I remember Rothesay being dubbed the 'Charing Cross of the Clyde steamboat services'. When I first went there in 1923 it was a very busy place, with the pier accommodating no fewer than five of the largest passenger vessels at once. Before the county boundaries were altered Rothesay was the county town of Bute, and the Prince of Wales has always had as one of his hereditary titles that of Duke of Rothesay. In regrouping days the North British Railway made a great feature of naming its express locomotives with resounding Scottish titles, and I have fond memories of a fine trip from Dundee up to Aberdeen, on the footplate of the *Duke of Rothesay* and how one of her regular drivers always called her, the gender for a steam locomotive was always feminine, 'the grand Old Duke'.

But this chapter is about ships, not locomotives, and before we get on to the main subject I must write something about some of the famous passenger ships that I saw, photographed, and travelled in on our month's stay at Rothesay. The paddle steamers of the former Caledonian and Glasgow and South Western railways had been merged under the LMS flag, with a not very attractive combined parti-coloured funnel. The LMS ships coming variously from Greenock (Princes Pier), from Gourock, Wemyss Bay, and Largs, were the most numerous, and among the privately owned shipping lines pride of place had inevitably to be given to the Royal Mail twin-funnelled paddle-steamer of the famous West Highland company, David MacBrayne, the *Columba*, which had carried the mails from Glasgow to various West Highland ports up to Ardrisaig unfailingly since 1878! She left Bridge Wharf in the heart of Glasgow at 7.11 a.m. each morning, and her sailing was the punctuality of a chronometer. The passenger steamers of the former North British Railway, then LNER, were based at Craigendoran, near Helensburgh, on the north of the Firth of Clyde. Their routes were mostly north of Rothesay, though they, with their red funnels, made a picturesque showing when they did arrive.

The North British Railway began building paddle steamers for working from Craigendoran pier in 1880, and they were all named after famous characters in the novels of Sir Walter Scott: *Ivanhoe* was the first, and then came *Madge Wildfire* and *Lucy Ashton*. By the 1890s traffic was increasing, and from the earlier steamers with their gross tonnages not much over 200 tons the size and carrying capacity increased until some of the later units built before the turn of the century were registered to carry well over one thousand passengers. So were added the *Talisman*, the *Kenilworth*, and largest of all in the North British fleet, the *Waverley*, licensed to carry no fewer than 1467 passengers. She was built in 1899. In 1952 writing of *The Firth of Clyde* from a lifetime's study and work George Blake, having eulogised the paddle steamers of the Glasgow and South Western Railway, went on to say 'The ships of the North British seemed somewhat nondescript and clumsy by comparison, though some of their later vessels, notable the *Waverley* of 1899, had both grace and speed.' I cannot say that I saw this particular ship in Rothesay though I was riding in her later on that same holiday.

Switching off to locomotives again briefly it would seem that the locomotive department of the North British followed the steamer people and got in on the act of using characters in the novels of Sir Walter Scott for a new class of express passenger engines introduced in 1909. But even before this, in 1906, one of the impressive new 'Atlantic' engines, for the heaviest express work on the line, had been named *Waverley*. However I have always had the impression that this engine was named after the Waverley station in Edinburgh and used on the romantically named Waverley Route through the Border country to Carlisle. Of the other steamers in the North British Railway fleet at Craigendoran there was no locomotive named *Marmion*. New engines named *Dandie Dinmont, Madge Wildfire,* and *Ivanhoe* were added to the stud in 1909, while further units of an improved version were the *Kenilworth* and the *Talisman*. It was not until after grouping of the British Railways in 1923 and the decision of the management of the newly formed London and North-Eastern Railway that a new batch of 4-4-0s of the former Great Central design should be sent to Scotland that these ultimately were given names of characters in the Waverley novels. One of these was the *Lucy Ashton,* and I was pleased to see she was to be our engine when I was travelling from Edinburgh to Perth one morning in late August 1927. The photograph I took before leaving Waverley station still adorns the pages of the log book concerned.

Now back to paddle-steamers on the Firth of Clyde, while in Rothesay we learned of a tour northwards from our immediate holiday pitch into the fjord-like recesses of Loch Long. It was a route exclusive to the North British vessels, with the solitary exception of the MacBrayne mail-boat *Iona* which went from Greenock to the piers in Loch Long and Loch Goil. She was a smaller version of the *Columba,* indistinguishable in outward appearance unless one saw them both together which few people ever did. The *Iona* had been built as early as 1864. At Rothesay I made some enquiries as to how we could get a trip in her, but her sailings did not match up with other workings on the Firth of Clyde. Even so, from Rothesay we could not directly connect with the North British steamer working on the Loch Long run. We had to take another steamer to Dunoon and there join one which had started from Craigendoran, and crossed to Gourock before heading true north into the dark, deep, and immeasurably alluring waters of Loch Long. When it arrived at Dunoon from Gourock I was interested to see we were to travel in the *Waverley,* the largest then of all the North British paddle-steamers.

So, after calling at Kirn, and Blairmore we headed into the wilds. The novelist George Blake has written: 'One of the startling paradoxes of travel in that region is to be encountered merely by driving a car out of the mild Gare Loch basin for a mile or two uphill and then find oneself, at Whistlefield, staring westward across the gloomy cleft of Loch Long into the mysteries of Loch Goil, and into an angry sunset over a range of crowded and eccentric peaks.' Then in one of my own books, *Scottish Railways*, I have written: 'The *Waverley* was forging her way up the narrow fjord of Loch Long. It was a gloriously fine autumn day; the keen mountain air was tempered by the warmth of the sun, and the quiet broken by the rhythmic "splash splash" of the paddles. My camera had to be continuously at the ready since leaving Dunoon, and on this my first trip into the region I was keeping a look-out for a glimpse of the West Highland Railway, which I knew ran somewhere on the hills to our right. As the steamer turned out of Loch Goil and headed north I was attracted by an engine whistle; and a moment later I saw the train – yes, the train! From the deck of the steamer it looked like a tiny "double-O" gauge model, and we watched it as it followed the curving track downhill, sometimes almost vanishing, then coming into full view, till it took the curve through Whistlefield and turned away downhill to Garelochhead'.

On that occasion one of our party remarked that it would be a marvellous ride up there in that train, though for my part it was another nine years before I travelled over that route, and then not in the best of circumstances for sightseeing. I was travelling in the sleeping-car express that left Fort William just after 5 p.m. and on a lowering September evening it was getting dark by the time we left Arrochar and started up the heavy gradient overlooking Loch Long which leads to Whistlefield. I must confess that on that occasion I was more concerned with clocking the mile posts rather than observing the darkening scenery over the loch. But apart from railways, George Blake gives some interesting details about oceanology of the region. Both Loch Long and Loch Goil are very deep. The former reaches a depth of 55 fathoms (330 ft.) near the entrance to Loch Goil, where the railway traveller looks down when passing Whistlefield station, while Loch Goil itself has a maximum depth of 47 fathoms (282 ft.).

The latter however has a bar at its entrance, over which the water level is only 7 fathoms deep (42 ft.). Oceanology apart Loch Goil and Loch Long provide some splendid sightseeing when the weather is fine, as it was on our family trip in 1923.

I took many photographs that day, at that time inevitably in monochrome. Moreover the films were not as colour conscious as they later became, and my pictures gave no more than the merest inkling of the glorious mountain scenery we had beheld. When I went to Arrochar at an Easter weekend more than twenty years later, and again took many photographs in monochrome, I was astonished at the difference the more sophisticated film made to my results. In all my pictures on the waterways of the Firth of Clyde, those of ships were almost always in the nature of portraits when they were closely approaching Rothesay pier or leaving it, and the majority of my other pictures were of mountain-scapes, with one or other of the waterways as a not too distinguished foreground – this because it was difficult to render the fascinating lights and shades on the constantly moving waters. I often tried to contrive a jetty or a small steamer pier to break up an otherwise featureless foreground. But cruising up Loch Long and Loch Goil in the *Waverley* that day, there were so many magnificent mountain scenes to photograph that I soon had no exposures left to finish the trip. I had nothing for the *Waverley* at any rate!

Then, in 1948, came the commission from Thomas Nelsons to write the book on *Scottish Railways*, and Ronnie Nelson, who was masterminding the job himself, wanted plenty of colour. It was not enough to have locomotives and trains; he suggested that one of the Clyde steamboats be included. I knew that he had some partiality towards the North British Railway, so I suggested painting one of the Craigendoran fleet; I had photographs of one or two of them taken at Rothesay in 1923 and then I stopped short. This particular issue was of momentous interest to me, because it contained the very first article of mine that was ever published: *Carlisle – a station of changes*. But far more appropriate in the present context was an article describing recent additions to the Clyde fleet of steamships, including new *Jennie Deans* which has recently taken the place of the veteran *Waverley* on the run up Loch Long and Loch Goil to Arrochar. More

The paddle-steamer Waverley, navigating stern-first from the pier at Lochgoilhead.

important still there was a photograph of the *Waverley* leaving Lochgoilhead. The author, then a well-known contributor to the magazine, was unlucky enough to have a day of lowering skies, though the profiles of the surrounding heights were clear. His picture did not include the pier itself though the composition was otherwise very pleasing.

I decided that this picture should be the basis of my steamship illustration in the Nelson book. Ronnie approved, but I was uncertain of the foreground – Langmuir's photograph in *The Railway Magazine* showed only a corner of the shore and I had no pictures of my own to refer to. In fact I cannot recollect getting off the steamer while the *Waverley* was berthed at Lochgoilhead, I had plenty of other photographs and so I sketched a composite picture expanding the background of the mountains in Langmuir's shot, making them look considerably more cheerful, and added the pier and some spectators to the foreground. Ronnie Nelson, whose knowledge of the West Highlands is profound, approved my draft sketch and so I went ahead. The printers made a super job of the reproduction and so it appeared as one of the fourteen colour plates in my book *Scottish Railways* which was published in 1950. The caption beneath the picture included this addendum: 'This fine old steamer, built 1899, was sunk in the Dunkirk evacuation'.

The book itself was kindly received and a new and revised edition was called for ten years later. The publishers asked for one of the colour plates of modern locomotives to be altered to show the changed colours that had been adopted by British Railways since the first edition was printed. This new version with its changes of colour on one plate provoked a friend who knew and loved all the Clyde steamers to write to me privately, in a humorous and sarcastic way to ask why, when the changing of the colour of that engine was done, why did you not scrap the old *Waverley* and put in a picture of her successor? That other ship, the beautiful *Jeanie Deans*, had taken over the Loch Long and Loch Goil run from the *Waverley* in 1931, having been built new in the previous autumn, specially for the job.

The *Jeanie Deans* is, because she is still in service today, though not often on the Firth of Clyde, still in service for excursion work. I wish my 'sarcastic' friends had written earlier for the *Jeanie Deans* is a very handsome paddle-steamer, considerably longer than the *Waverley*, and having two funnels. In the books to which reference is made here, both authorities in their respective spheres disagree as to her dimensions and carrying capacity, so I will not quote either of them here, beyond saying that apparently the *Jeanie Deans* did not accommodate many more passengers than the *Waverley*, 'that old thing' as my sarcastic friend called her! The *Jeanie Deans*, despite her modern design did not carry anything like the numbers officially registered to the famous MacBrayne mail-boat *Columba*, which could carry nearly 2200 people if necessary. Those Clyde paddle-steamers took their loads. The old *Waverley* was registered to carry about 1400!

Chapter 13

The mid-morning Southbound Express from Inverness by Culloden Moor

Early in the year 1927, the family much to my surprise and delight decided that for the whole of my father's month of annual leave from the Bank they would be going into the Highlands of Scotland. The million-dollar question was, where? My mother was always the dominant factor in making such decisions. She never ceased to be Victorian in her attitude to holidays. The chosen place must have a sea 'front', preferably with a promenade, with seats where one could recline at one's leisure, doze off, or even knit! When I went home for the Easter break the family had not got much farther than some preliminary ideas, but I must say I did some prodding to them to get on with their plans, in view of my mother's invariable insistence that we had private apartments, and full board and lodging, even though she had to do most of the shopping herself.

When I went north for the next holiday break, at Whitsun, I found the house was deluged in travel brochures, guide books and such like. The local manager of Thomas Cook & Sons was a Bank customer of my father's and he, learning of the family's intentions, seemed keen to send us as far as possible, rail mileage-wise from Barrow. They had decided on Nairn, overlooking the Moray Firth. In readiness for my own visit, in the middle fortnight of their stay at the end of August, I bought an Ordnance Survey Map; though not one-inch this time, but of the reduced scale, two miles to the inch to cover a larger area. Anticipating being based in Nairn I began to map out excursions that the family might take by train and hired car to see as much of the country as possible. But there was also the matter of railway photography on the Highland Line. It was only four years since the original Highland Railway had been incorporated in the LMS system, and while I believed that the older locomotives had been painted in new colours I understand that there was not much change otherwise. I began making arrangements for my bicycle to go up to Nairn with me when the time came round. Judging from my studies of the map there were good roads to some of the most likely places to get interesting photographs.

When holiday time came round my parents had gone up by a night train, and I also went from London to Edinburgh by night. I myself paused in the Scots capital city for breakfast and then went on by the morning express which carried through carriages for the loop line to Inverness via Forres, and which landed me in Nairn just before afternoon tea-time. But I had not been long in Scotland before I found that 'tea', including anything up to a steak and chips, could be served any time up to ten o'clock in the evening! My parent's lodgings, I found, were some little from the 'front' as it was. Actually there were no houses at all near the shore, for obvious reasons as I was to learn later. But there was a pleasant path above the shingle of the beach itself, and which we all used on occasions. On my first evening at Nairn the weather was brilliant, and I was entranced by the outlook northwards across the Moray Firth. In this weather we could see the coastline as far as the mountains of Caithness-shire, beyond Helmsdale, where the Highland main line turned inland and from the sea. I looked forward, sometime, to a trip on the farthest north railway in Britain, but not this holiday. The journey from Inverness to Wick took the best part of a whole day.

My railway activities this time were mainly on photography, and before leaving London I had studied the timetables and there were three important through expresses leaving Inverness by the direct line to the south, not going through Nairn, in the late afternoon. The first of the three was a purely Scottish service carrying a travelling post-office carriage throughout from Helmsdale to Perth and through carriages from Inverness to Glasgow and Edinburgh. This left the Highland capital at 3.45 p.m. Next, at 4.15 p.m., was the West Coast sleeping car express for Euston, and finally at 4.35 p.m. came the combined sleeping car express for both West and East Coast routes to London, always a very heavy train, and divided at Perth to proceed separately on the once deadly rival routes to the south. With the aid of my Ordnance Survey map I picked the way to ride to Culloden Moor station, about ten miles run from Nairn. The LMS people in Scotland had given me walking permits for the entire distance, by both routes, between Inverness and Aviemore, so on my first trip, when the weather was fine, I parked my bicycle at Culloden Moor station and set off up the line.

The direct line south from Inverness starts from little more than sea level on the shores of the Ness estuary and in only $22\frac{1}{2}$ miles it had climbed to an altitude of 1315 feet in the Slochd Mhuic pass. The average gradient throughout is thus 1 in 93, but particularly near the start there are some solid blocks of ascent on 1 in 60. On the other hand on the stretch where I was now beginning my walk there is a rapid descent to the crossing of the river Nairn, with it's magnificent stone viaduct. I had not gone far when, looking back, I saw the signals had been pulled off for an up train. It proved a relief to the mail, hauled by the *Clan Mackinnon*, then painted in Midland red, and going well. In the summer tourist season, all the regular trains were very heavy, and as the maximum load permitted to be hauled unassisted by the powerful and efficient 4-6-0s of the Highland Railway over this gruelling first stage of the journey southwards from Inverness was 220 tons, double-heading was almost always needed with all three trains. The unassisted loading limit had, of necessity, to be kept rather less than the locomotives could haul in the ordinary way because the train engines were starting 'cold' from Inverness, and the ascent of a 1 in 60 is hardly the place to be if the fire is a bit 'green'!

I found the locomotive people at Inverness had developed an ingenious way of helping the engine crews of units working through to Perth, or sometimes even to Glasgow while their engines were getting warmed up in the terrific ascent out of Inverness. Three connecting trains arrived in the early afternoon, the first from points east, Nairn, Forres, Elgin, Keith and the GNS line. Then came the

Hebridean boat train from the Kyle of Lochalsh, bringing passengers from many remote spots in the Western Isles. Finally there was the North Mail, through from Wick, with the T.P.O. carriage from Helmsdale to be transferred to the 3.45 p.m. for the south. The Keith train always had a 4-4-0, usually a 'Loch' or a 'Small Ben', and this was used to pilot the Euston 'sleeper' which usually was the least heavy of the three. The engine from the Kyle was usually a goods 4-6-0, one of the historic Jones type, or one of the later superheated Cumming design, though one day when I was photographing near Loch Luichart, in Rosshire the train came up headed by a resplendent Skye Bogie 4-4-0. I have often wondered if she was put to the usual piloting turn south of Inverness that day, on the 3.45 p.m. Mail. The engine from Wick was always a 'Castle', and it was used on the 4.35 p.m., usually the heaviest train of the three. On this first outing I photographed all three trains and then walked back to the station to collect my bicycle. I then took the road over the moor itself, past the battlefield of 1745, keeping the line in sight across the valley and looking out for further photographic viewpoints. Then, too far to get a picture, I saw the fascinating sight of the three pilot engines, coupled together and of course tender-first, drifting down the steep gradient and heading for Inverness.

I was back to our lodgings at Nairn that evening. No matter where we stayed my mother always insisted on having 'Nursery Tea' about five o'clock, and the lady in whose house we were staying, a Mrs Ross, had remarked upon my absence on that particular day. Mother told her that I had gone to Culloden Moor taking photographs. Mrs Ross was curious, asked what subjects were there in that locality, other than the grim reminders of the battle. When my mother told her that I had gone there to photograph trains the Scots lady, far from being surprised, was thrilled to bits. For it transpired that her father was Stationmaster at Nairn for many years and that she lived in the station house before she was married. More than that, one day she went to a cupboard in one of her rooms and brought out a whole collection of *Railway Magazines* dating between 1906 and 1913. Treasure trove indeed for me, because I had not been able to afford such interesting back numbers. After their own holiday my father took the individual numbers back to Barrow and had them bound

for me. They are still on my bookshelves now. In 1927 I made a
second visit to the Direct Line, parking my bicycle at Daviot station
and photographing the same series of afternoon expresses, and with
a pleasing variety of ex-Highland Railway locomotives. The holiday
was generally voted a great success and before my parents left they
had booked up with Mrs Ross for a further visit, in August 1928.

Before I went north again I had learned that the six 'River' class
4-6-0s which had been banned from the Highland Railway in the
fiasco of 1915, had been restored to their ancestral home and were
working between Perth and Inverness. There were, I gathered, certain other developments in the motive power department of which I
was made immediately aware when I travelled north on the 12 noon
express from Perth, *en route* for Nairn. At summer weekends it was
always a very heavy train, with through portions from Glasgow and
Edinburgh for both the direct and the Forres line to Inverness and a
Pullman dining car conveyed as far as Aviemore. In 1927 we had been
hauled by two 'Clan' class 4-6-0s from Perth, but a year later, while the
train engine which took the Forres line portion forward from Aviemore was also a 'Clan', the pilot engine was a Midland Class 4 0-6-0
goods, and she made a great deal of noise doing the job. I did not see
any of the 'Rivers' on this journey northward, but once estab-lished at
Nairn I made an early trip to Inverness to study the form. I went on
the afternoon train from Keith and found the curiously arranged
terminal station very busy. The mail was already in from Wick and its
southern continuation was running into two sections, the first taking
the T.P.O. carriage and the Glasgow portion, and the second the
Edinburgh and additional coaches for local passengers. On the first
part, a 'River' was the train engine, and in this I embarked for the trip
to Aviemore, for some photographic work on the line.

I was pleased to see our train engine was still in the red livery
adopted for all passenger engines when the LMS was formed. In
1928 I was sorry to see that some of the Highland 'Clans' had been
re-painted in plain black. The shed staff evidently voiced their disgust at this move by refusing to clean them at all. On the up mail as
far as Slochd summit we had the *Clan Chattan* as pilot, and it was
filthy! At Aviemore the 'River', it should have been *River Tay* originally, but the intended names were not used when the use of these

engines on the Highland was banned in 1915, continued unassisted with the Mail, and I got one of my best ever photographs of a moving train as she was leaving, with a spectacular smoke effect. I took many more photographs at Aviemore that day, before returning to Inverness and catching the last train for Nairn. The weather was not so good as in the previous year and my cycling expeditions less frequent. But on one promising day I rode out to Culloden Moor to photograph the mid-morning south express. That arch-priest of rail photographers, F E Mackay, always said that trains seen from outer side of a curve were never satisfactory because only the engine and the first few coaches were seen. But he was never a pictorialist, and concentrated on giving the clearest impression of a train at speed. He would never have attempted a shot on the immediately south side of Culloden Viaduct!

The train I was intent on photographing was due to pass at about 11.15 a.m. and knowing my mother's insistence on punctuality at meal times, particularly at midday, I had no time to ride to seek a further viewpoint. It was 'Hobson's Choice', the outside of that curve! When the train called briefly at Culloden Moor station I could see it was hauled by two 4-6-0 locomotives, and the train engine looked like a 'River'. They got smartly away on the steep descending gradient to the viaduct and they were doing about 40 m.p.h. when they came to my viewpoint – *Brahan Castle* leading. The 'River' was the first of the six to be built, originally the *River Ness*, and one of the only two to be painted in the handsome green livery used on Highland engines at that time. When I 'shot' that train in 1928 I am glad that both engines were still in Midland red, with their five-figure numbers in huge figures on their tenders, 14687 and 14756; *Brahan Castle* was one of the engines I had 'timed' on my previous visit to Scotland in 1927. She had one of the inside framed double-bogie tenders that Peter Drummond introduced following his elder brother, Dugald's use of them on the London and South Western Railway.

The resulting photograph, though clear and enabling the numbers of the two engines to be discerned was not one of my favourites. I printed it, contact, and put it into one of my albums and there it stayed. The album is still on my shelves and the print, though proc-

On the Highland Line in 1928: the mid-morning southbound express from Inverness near Culloden Moor.

essed 64 years ago, is showing no sign of deterioration today. In my student days I used to do all my own developing and printing when I was home at Barrow for the long university holidays. I must admit I have not the slightest recollection of the circumstances that led to the water colour that forms the centre-piece of this chapter. It is dated 1942, in the middle of World War II, when we were living in Chippenham, and our son had been born. Now I have been carefully through my writings at that time, and there is still not a clue! The picture is a most faithful copy of the photograph, though not quite to the extent where *Brahan Castle* was leaking steam at the front end. It recalls a pleasant sunny morning with the moorland on which the battle of 1745 was fought providing an interesting background. While the 'Rivers' have always been one of my favourite classes of British locomotives I am still wondering why, when it came to a painting, I did not pick on the shot of the sister engine leaving Aviemore with the up Mail.

All the same I am glad that the two engines I photographed that day were in the 'red' livery and not the unspeakable black which earned the utmost disgust from all the Highland enginemen and shed staff. It is true I photographed one of them, that day I had at Aviemore, that had been repainted, but it must have been a recent repair because the engine in question, No. 14759, had not got to the stage of filth as some of the 'Clans' I saw in that same summer. The 'Rivers', or at any rate the first two of them must surely constitute the only British locomotive class of pre-grouping origin that have been painted in four different colours. I expect that few people saw *River Ness* and *River Spey* on their first arrival at Perth from the builder's works on Tyneside, nor when they were taken ignominiously for alteration to their chimneys to St Rollox. Then they were painted Highland green. They emerged painted in Caledonian blue, looking very fine, I believe, though I never saw one of them at this time. I learned that they were used mostly on long distance express goods trains, and kept looking very smart. Then these engines were successively green, blue, red and 'lamp black'. When my large model railway at Silver Cedars, High Bannerdown, needed some additional express passenger engine power I had a Highland 'River' built, and finished in the original style. I chose No. 73 *River Findhorn*, because the glen in which that river ran had given me some of the most beautiful scenes that were ever presented to my camera. Also the engine I had photographed in black at Aviemore, No. 14759, should by rights have been the *River Findhorn*.

Chapter 14
Dartmoor, hunting antiquities, Fingle Bridge

I think my first interest in seeking out relics that remain in Great Britain of a civilization far older than that covered in the ordinary history books goes back to my first visit to Penzance in the late summer of 1924. At Imperial College in London I had just got a degree in Engineering, but my father had decided to give me a post-graduate year, and so I was enjoying my last college vacation, and I was with my parents for the entire month of their stay in Cornwall. We stayed at a pleasant private apartments house on the sea front, with a sitting room commanding a glorious view over the entire sweep of Mounts Bay. But the evenings were closing in by the end of August, and I was glad to find our hostess had some interesting topographical books on her shelves. One of them particularly took my fancy. It was a book describing in detail some of the interesting features of the Land's End district, not only beauty spots but the various prehistoric relics that could be seen. With a month's stay at my disposal, and my bicycle ready at hand, I made for the prehistoric sights as keenly as I walked the coastal cliff paths, and, tell it not in Gath, the linesides of the Great Western Railway!

I photographed the spectacular Dolmen known as Lanyon Quoit, an easy morning's ride from Penzance, and spent much time the same evening looking up its origin, which I gathered dated from Neolithic days, around 3000 years BC! From this particular guide book I discovered that there were several other Quoits in the Land's End area, though none so ready accessible as Lanyon. But with plenty of time at my disposal I sought out Chun Quoit near St Just, Mulfra, and Zennor and I photographed them all. They were far from the roads, and some of them took some finding, but I entered into the spirit of the search and it proved well worth it, even though the Quoits were far less spectacular than that of Lanyon. Back in London for the last of my years at Imperial College I was asked to give a lantern lecture on my visit to West Cornwall, and I had to do some intensive reading up to make my observations on those antiquities intelligible to my audience. Fortunately they were a relatively small part of the story I had to tell, and display on the screen.

Lantern lectures apart, my interest in these neolithic antiquities was well and truly aroused, and when the family decided on Paignton for my father's annual holiday from the Bank in 1925 I began to look up Dartmoor, where I had heard there were plenty more of these relics. The only trouble now was that the days of my long college vacations were ended. At the end of July I was being enrolled as a Graduate-Trainee at Westinghouse, and I could only spare two weeks with my parents at Paignton. But the weather was glorious and what with photographing the beautiful scenic coastline of Torbay, the Dart estuary, and the villages around, to say nothing of frequent visits to the Great Western main line, which provided a rich variety of smartly cleaned-up locomotives, the fortnight went all too quickly, even though I had my bicycle on hand to provide transport for nearly all my excursions. For this year Dartmoor and its antiquities were having to be given a miss, particularly as they were mostly out of range on a push-bicycle trip from Paignton. The consensus of opinion in our family circle was that we should make for Paignton for holidays also in the following year.

By the late spring of that year my training had taken me to the Westinghouse Works at Chippenham, Wiltshire where I was in lodgings with a pleasant couple, he an old servant of the company and she a good housekeeper, though unhappily childless. The weather at that time was not very good, and I spent a lot of time reading. I had purchased the famous book on Dartmoor by the Revd S Baring-Gould, and I was fascinated by his vivid accounts of the history, antiquities, and folklore of the Moor. In my spare moments 'in digs' I planned out a number of excursions for the time when I could join my parents at Paignton, at the end of August. The only difficulty was that these trips would have to be done by hired cars. Neither my father or my mother could drive and although I myself had a licence I was not then an experienced enough driver to tackle the hills and dales of Dartmoor. Fortunately during their previous stay at Paignton they had made contact with a car-hire firm which had provided them with a few short trips and their drivers were ready enough to go further afield.

The only trouble with these chaps was that Dartmoor meant only two recognised excursions, either to Widdecombe-in-the-Moor, to see the site of the legendary 'Fair' or to Princetown, to catch a glimpse of the convicts at work! It was another matter altogether when one of the passengers had a one-inch to the mile Ordnance Survey map with him and was intent on piloting the hapless driver into country unknown to him, or to any of his colleagues, yet less than 30 miles from their home base. One of the first expeditions on Dartmoor was to see not an antiquity from an old-age past civilization such as had interested me in Cornwall, but a gigantic freak of nature. The weathering of the granite tops of many of the moorland heights resulted in characteristic cappings, or 'tors' as they are known in the West Country, but my local guide book, and of course Baring-Gould's fine book, pinpointed another, which very much excited my curiosity and interests. Baring-Gould quotes Carrington, thus:

'On the very edge
Of the vast moorland, startling every eye,
A shape enormous rises! High it towers
Above the hill's bold brow, and seen from far,
Assumes the human form; a granite god, –
To whom, in days long flown, the suppliant knee
In trembling homage bow'd'

In less poetic language Baring-Gould adds: 'It stands up, a core of hard granite, forty feet high, in five layers above a 'clitter', the softest masses that have fallen off from it. Had it ever been venerated as an idol, the worshippers would assuredly have done something towards clearing this clitter away, so as to give themselves a means of easy access to their idol, and some turf on which to kneel in adoration.' I had previously pinpointed the site of the Bowerman's Nose, near to the summit of Hayne Down, about a mile southeast of the little village of Manaton, uphill from the valley of the river Bovey. It was right off the beaten tracks of normal sightseeing on Dartmoor, far from the main road from Newton Abbot to Moretonhampsted and the erstwhile branch line of the Great Western Railway. We had to diverge at Bovey Tracey and make our way by winding and hilly roads to Manaton village. Then came the real crunch! From the lanes west of the village a track, ominously uncoloured on my Ordnance Map, led up to Hayne Down, and I pointed the way to one very unwilling driver. For an object eventually as prominent as Bowerman's Nose it was singularly hard to find, and we had no end of a chase – a chase that was no doubt retold in all the pubs in Paignton, where our driver visited. I got a good photograph of it, and painted the scene in water-colours, though I cannot tell now where the picture went.

On the day when we went searching for the Bowerman's Nose the weather was clear and we got some fine prospects over the eastern uplands of Dartmoor, but the outlook generally was not anything like so good as it had been in the month the family had enjoyed at Paignton in the previous summer. On the next day when we had booked up a car for another expedition on to Dartmoor the skies were lowering at breakfast time, though the forecast did not foretell rain. So off we went, with a different driver. Nevertheless the grapevine had been at work, and the second man was occasionally taking sidelong glances towards the Ordnance Survey maps I was carrying. We headed west from Paignton on this particular day, through Totnes and as far as Ivybridge on the main road to Plymouth because I wanted to explore some of the more westerly parts of Dartmoor. So, from Ivybridge we began to climb. The skies had continued lowering, but when we got further uphill we entered a region of dense wet mist and we could see nothing at all – barely one car's length ahead of us! We stopped, and thereupon decided that Dartmoor was definitely 'not on' for that day. We had plenty of sustenance for a full day's trip, and having returned to Ivybridge we headed south for Kingsbridge and Salcombe, and had a pleasant day, though not a good one for taking photographs, because of the poor light. Still the rain held off until evening.

On the edge of Dartmoor: Fingle Bridge, where the River Teign has emerged from the moorland fastnesses.

I was very intrigued by the use of the word 'Cyclopean', in Old English lettering, on some of the bridges in the heart of Dartmoor in my Ordnance Survey Maps. Baring-Gould does not use the word at all, but looking it up in the dictionary I found it referred to 'a prehistoric style of masonry with immense stones of irregular form'. The so-called 'Clapper Bridge' at Postbridge crossing the East Dart River in the very heart of the moor certainly looks like this. There is another one at the junction of the East and West Dart rivers, at Dartmeet, though one of the huge cap-stones has in this instant been dislodged. We saw both these Cyclopean bridges, and I duly photographed the one at Postbridge on our way to the hamlet of Merrivale about two miles west of Princetown, which we carefully avoided by taking the almost straight road which runs from Two Bridges towards Tavistock. Before reaching Merrivale itself there was a fine example of a prehistoric Stone Avenue, which Batsford's 'Guide to Prehistoric England' dates from the Bronze Age, more than 1000 years BC. This relic can be seen easily from the main road and I found it an enjoyable walk across the moorland to take some photographs at close range. In Cornwall, in the Land's End district, I had photographed some of the small stone circles, but on Dartmoor, one of the finest (so my guide book told me); 'The Grey Wethers' was 2¼ miles across the moor from Postbridge, with no track or otherwise pointing the way. I did not risk this, leaving the car and my parents for an hour or so tramp in the heather. The guide books tell me the two circles have respective diameters of 103¼ and 116½ ft., with 15 stones in one circle and 27 in the other.

On the case-bound cover of Baring-Gould's book, beautifully finished with the title, author and publisher in gilt on the spine, there was an accurate representation, also in gilt, of the only surviving dolmen in the Dartmoor region, the 'Spinster's Rock' some two miles west of Drewsteignton, and in the high country north of the Teign Valley. On one of our trips we found this fine monument and photographed it, and while in the relatively near neighbourhood I guided our driver down the precipitous slope to the crossing of the River Teign in the Fingle Gorge, which Lady Northcote considered to be the most beautiful of the many beautiful glens through which the Teign passes. I cannot better her loving description, thus: 'It is a deep ravine with high and steep sides, that are thickly wooded and broken by great boulders. At Fingle Bridge four winding valleys meet; that is, the combe down which the river sweeps from above curves one way, and the narrow opening into which it disappears twists sharply round in another. A cleft, half hidden in trees, divides the line of hills that shut in the tiny valley meadow on the west, and a road and a small stream scramble down a less severe descent between the high sides, from the north-east. But from no point near the bridge would it be more possible to see far up any cleeve, than it would be for a ladybird, perched at one end, to trace all the lines of a stag's horn . . .'

I took several photographs, although the confined location did not help. I felt as though an aerial viewpoint would be needed to give full justice to the beauty of the place. However one of my pictures caught the eyes of the rest of the family and they had it enlarged and made into Christmas cards, albeit in monochrome. About a year later I painted the picture in water-colour, in an attempt to get some colour into my 'digs'-encircled life in Central London!

In her book, Lady Northcote mentions some historic sites on both sides of the Teign Gorge, but as neither of these involved more than earthworks dating roughly from the early British occupation, and conflicts with the Roman invaders I gave them a 'miss', except that one of them went by the name of 'Cranbrook Castle'! As a railway enthusiast, and photographer of trains in motion, I was of course aware that the Great Western Railway was naming some of the latest and most powerful express passenger locomotives after castles; but these were historic national monuments like Windsor, Warwick and Caerphilly, not prehistoric mounds of earth. Even so, as the stock of names, and the output of new engines from Swindon increased rapidly, some less familiar titles adorned the handsome nameplates of the Great Western express locomotives, though I was surprised to see, in August 1936, that the engine hauling the 5.15 p.m. train from Bristol was the *Cranbrook Castle*. She was then brand new, in spanking condition, and gave us a magnificent run to Paddington, running many miles east of Reading at well over 80 m.p.h.

But the engine in question, No. 5048, did not carry the name for long. One of the independent Welsh railways taken over by the Great

Western in the amalgamations of 1923 was the Cambrian, and although running a passenger service to coastal resorts like Barmouth and Aberystwyth, its track was not substantial enough to carry the weight of larger express locomotives, and older types had to be conditioned for the purpose. Because of the Welsh interest the publicity department of the G.W.R. hit on the idea of naming these reconditioned 4-4-0s after Earls, many of which had Welsh associations. But the process of naming had not gone far before some of the noble lords concerned objected to their names being used on such relatively insignificant engines and arrangements had to be made for them to be transferred to engines of the Castle class. So in 1937, engine No. 5048 *Cranbrook Castle* became *Earl of Devon.* I saw it many times, and often travelled behind it in its new guise, while the nameplates were not long in store. A further batch of Castles were built at Swindon in 1938, and of these No. 5073 was allocated to *Cranbrook Castle.*

This new engine however did not bear the name much longer than did its predecessor, for the war came and with it the Battle of Britain, and in the spirit of grateful patriotism of the time the Great Western Railway felt that some of their principal express locomotives should be named after the aircraft and their crews who had done so much for the Allied cause. In January 1941 engine No. 5073 was renamed *Blenheim,* and it continued running on the North to West services from Shrewsbury to Newton Abbot via the Severn Tunnel. Although construction of further engines of the 'Castle' class was recommenced at Swindon after the war it was not until 1950, in the final batch built under British Railways management, that the name *Cranbrook Castle* was used again, on engine No. 7030. It was stationed for a time, I believe, at Worcester and performed on some fine runs notably between Oxford and Paddington. Then when dieselization began, as a relatively new engine *Cranbrook Castle* the third was not scrapped but put into store. By that time it had been modernized by having a twin-orifice blastpipe and double chimney.

Then, early in 1962, proposals were in hand for accelerating the Paddington-Birmingham service and the civil engineer required a high-speed run with the 'whitewash' car to observe the condition of the track. For some reason that I cannot now recall the special was required to be steam hauled, and *Cranbrook Castle* was taken out of store from Old Oak Common sheds and prepared for the job. The chosen day was a Sunday 15 May 1962. Because of the very hard work that was anticipated, two firemen were carried, as well as the locomotive inspector on the footplate. They made the fastest runs ever recorded on that route, including two separate maximum speeds of 103 m.p.h. on the return journey. After this achievement however *Cranbrook Castle* went back into storage. She was scrapped only nine months later!

Chapter 15
Scottish Railways – Coats of Arms

About the end of World War II in connection with my Locomotive Performance articles in the magazine *Railways*, a correspondence started with a man writing from an address in Edinburgh who signed himself R I Nelson. He was evidently knowledgeable on the subject of train running north of Newcastle on the East Coast route and I began to use some of his notes in my articles. Correspondence blossomed, and then he invited me to meet him for dinner when he was in London. In due course an appointment was arranged, and then I discovered he was the Deputy Chairman of the famous Scottish and world-wide publishing firm of Thomas Nelson and Sons, whose works and head offices were in Edinburgh. He told me that they were about to publish a new book on Scotland, a description of Scotland itself and Scottish Life. Would I like to do a companion volume on Scottish Railways? Could a duck swim! There were nevertheless many considerations to be weighed up before accepting this very tempting pro- posal, but in no time a contract was drawn up. The year was then 1948. British railways had then been nationalized and the newly established Scottish Region, and their officers, were eager and willing to give me every facility I liked to ask for to amass data for the book.

At the beginning of May that year I took a week of my annual leave from Westinghouse to visit Scotland again. To meet in person some of the officers of Scottish Region to whom I was indebted for so many facilities, to travel on routes when I had never been before, including from Dingwall up to Wick, and to call in at Nelson's works on my way south. At his bachelor flat in central Edinburgh Ronald Nelson arranged a cocktail party for me to meet socially the half-dozen or so senior officers of the firm, male and female, who would be dealing with the editing and production of my book. It was an odd gathering. None of the people who had been summoned seemed to be on intimate relations with him. It was all very formal and 'correct'; no second drinks were offered, and if they had been I am sure they would not have been accepted! I found that all correspondence over my book was dealt with personally by Ronald Nelson himself. Those who came to the party dropped immediately from my ken. Of course the illustrations were to be a big feature, and I was rather concerned at his proposal – nay remit? – that there would be fourteen colour plates but only sixteen plates in monochrome! I tried to persuade him to alter this, but he was completely unyielding. He knew of my adventures in water colours and he commissioned me to paint pictures of Highland LMS and LNER trains in motion, while the paintings of certain stationary locomotives were entrusted to another artist.

Then the question came up of railway heraldry. We both felt that the demise of the old independent companies should have some memento in a book on Scottish Railways and we jointly conceived the idea of a plate embodying not only those of the newly-defunct LMS and LNER, but also those of the constituent pre-grouping companies. This was easier said than done. In the January 1948 issue of *The Railway Magazine* George Dow had written a copiously illustrated article on railway coats of arms, but of course at that time there was no colour. I had the almost forgotten part-work of 1910 vintage *Our Home Railways* which included colour plates of the Caledonian and North British devices. Those gave me a start, and when I went up to Scotland for my first tour on Nelson's behalf I obtained permission to see the magnificent Puller collection then housed in the Station Hotel, at Perth. I had Dow's article in my luggage and made as many notes as I needed on the actual colours of the Highland, Glasgow and South Western, and Great North of Scotland devices. Dow's article did not include any reference or illustration of the G & S.W.R. crest, so my visit to Perth was doubly important for my immediate task. I finished the paintings and Ronald Nelson sent them off to the Scottish Region of British Railways for their approval before block-making proceeded, and I am glad they passed without comment. In the Nelson book there was no time or space for any comments on the coat of arms, but the frontispiece of the book itself received honourable mention in some of the subsequent reviews.

My association with railway coats of arms came to the fore some dozen years later, when the Blandford Press asked me to follow my *Pocket Encyclopedia of British Steam Locomotives* with another dealing rather generally with the railway scene in Great Britain. As before there would be upwards of 190 colour plates, and these were to include the coats of arms of all the railways. This time there were to be explanatory notes as well, and for these I had to do a considerable amount of research. My 'labours of love', so indeed they proved in the case of the Scottish companies, proved very interesting, and they provide a pleasant accompaniment to the present exercise. Starting with the Caledonian, a study of the coat of arms, carried on engines and carriages alike, would suggest that it was a nationally-owned concern, because this insignia consisted of nothing more or less than the Royal arms of Scotland, with the Royal mottos included. Heraldically this device was without any justification, and probably without authority too! But in assuming this magnificent device the Caledonian was perpetuating a crucial point in its history. It was not by any means the first railway in Scotland, and its origin was the subject of acute controversy. The conception of a trunk line from Carlisle to Glasgow came from the Grand Junction Railway, and Scottish sentiment resented a project that had its origin in England! Nevertheless many far-seeing Scots backed it wholeheartedly, while others were equally strong in their opposition. But to conceal the English influences in its origin the name Caledonian was chosen.

In the nineteenth century, and indeed for some years afterwards, it was quite usual to refer to Scotland as 'North Britain' and letters from England addressed to Scottish towns and villages had the letters 'NB' added in addition to the normal address. The title 'North British Railway' could thus be construed as equally all-embracing as that of 'Caledonian'; and the two railways certainly had almost equal claims to be considered the premier line of Scotland. Originally it extended no further than from Edinburgh to Berwick-on-Tweed, and it is the arms of these two places that were embodied in its coat of arms, together with the thistle and the rose. Eventually the North British grew to include many other lines, including the continuation of the East Coast Main Line via the Forth and Tay bridges to Dundee and Aberdeen. It incorporated the Edinburgh and Glasgow Railway, and eventually the far-famed West Highland to Fort William, and its breathtaking extension to Mallaig, within sight of the great mountains of Skye. But the line originally built to link up Edinburgh and Berwick-on-Tweed never changed its name, and the engines and carriages of the twentieth century still carried the original coat of arms with the insignia of those two places within the encircling garter.

The Highland Railway was formed in 1865 by an amalgamation of the Inverness and Nairn, the Inverness and Aberdeen Junction, and the Inverness and Perth Junction railways. Naturally the overriding purpose of the promoters of this merger was to provide direct communication between Inverness and Perth, and this is symbolized in the coat of arms, including that of the city of Perth, and that of the burgh of Inverness. Both are remarkable devices in themselves. That of Perth consists of the Holy Lamb, carrying the banner of St Andrew, a device frequently used for public houses having the more prosaic name of 'The Lamb and Flag'. The arms of the burgh of Inverness depicts Our Lord upon the Cross, and thus both shields in the Highland Railway coat of arms have a deeply religious flavour. It was not until comparatively late in the company's history that this striking coat of arms was used on any locomotives. Then it was only those introduced by Christopher Cumming, after the sad episode of the 'River' Class and the precipitate departure of their designer, that the crest was introduced, on three new 4-6-0s of the 'Castle' class, on the two 4-4-0s designed specially for the North Mails between Inverness and Wick, and on the eight 'Clans'.

There has always been some doubt, particularly in the mind of enthusiasts who live south of the Border, as to what the true colour of the Highland locomotives was, after Peter Drummond dispensed with the elaborate lining and painting in his first years at Inverness. It seemed to 'weather' to shades varying between a rather shabby olive to a well groomed and polished blackish-blue-green. The latter shade was used by the artist who did the colour-plate of one of the

'Clan' class engines in the Nelson book that I wrote. Ronald Nelson, from his experience of all eight of them when they were working on the Oban line in the 1930s, decided that the *Clan Mackinnon* should be the one depicted. Of course he was too young to have seen any of them in their Highland Railways days, and he would not have known that the last four, built in 1921, were painted a much lighter green. I saw and photographed *Clan Mackinnon* when it and *Clan Chattan* were regularly working between Inverness and Glasgow on a double-home basis in the first year of the grouping. It looked magnificent. The colour background within the garter on the Highland coat of arms reflected the particular shade to which the engines had been painted. The five introduced by Cumming in 1917 were dark green and also were the first 'Clans'. This is the colour shown in the Meadway painting of the coat of arms in the Bladford colour book. But in my own rendering in the plate now reproduced, for the painting used in the Nelson book, I used the true 'Lochgorm green', which was a lovely deep moss green, quite rich in its *depth*. I have a fine example of it on the actual coat of arms that hangs in my present library.

The Great North of Scotland was once described as the little railway with the high-sounding name, which actually operated only in the north-eastern corner of the country. Its basis and headquarters were in Aberdeen, whence it was originally planned to reach Inverness. But from Aberdeen it had a most important branch line up Deeside, as far as Ballater, and when Queen Victoria and her successors were in residence at Balmoral Castle the line was often under Royal patronage. This undoubtedly led to the adoption of the rather grand coat of arms for such a relatively small railway. Aberdeen, of course, was the focal point of the system and it is the city arms, consisting of the three silver towers, that figure in two out of the four corners of the shield. The alternative quarters bear the lion rampant of Scotland. It is definitely known that this design was never registered at the College of Herald, nor submitted to Lord Lyon. Had it been submitted one feels it would have stood a good chance of rejection, through use of part of the Royal arms of Scotland. The locomotives of the GNSR never carried the coat of arms, colourful as they were otherwise. The green livery in which they were decked was quite distinctive from all the other shades of green used on pre-grouping British locomotives, bright, though not quite approaching the vivid 'malachite' adopted in Bulleid's day on the Southern Railway.

The Glasgow and South Western, unlike the two other Scottish railways which had main line connections across the Border, started its operation as a purely local concern, albeit a very important one, named the Glasgow, Paisley, Kilmarnock and Ayr Railway. Its extent was exactly that. But when certain influential interests were anxious for it to be extended southwards to Carlisle and provide a rival Anglo-Scottish route to that of the Caledonian from Glasgow, the original GPK & A changed its title to that of Glasgow and South Western. The emblem of the original company was eventually adopted, though not at any time displayed on locomotives or other rolling stock. At one time a very much more elaborate coat of arms was considered, and fortunately a copy, probably the only one originally painted for submission to the Board of the Railway company, was in the Puller collection. It was reproduced in the Centenary publications of the Stephenson Locomotive Society to mark the event in 1950. It is a very elaborate affair with the device eventually used by the G & SWR surrounded by lions and the armorial crests of Glasgow, Greenock, Paisley, Ayr, Dumfries, Kilmarnock, Girvan, Carlisle and Sanquhar. I have never seen it personally but from the photograph it looks a most impressive affair. The actual coat of arms of the G & SWR was not included nor illustrated in George Dow's article in *The Railway Magazine* and when I was doing the work for my Nelson book I had to rely entirely on my own observations in the Station Hotel at Perth.

The device eventually adopted, though not displayed to any extent on any of the company's equipment or property, was that of the parent system, that of the GPK & A, because it was considered to be equally appropriate to the enlarged company. The three devices banded together by the crown, and encircled by the traditional garter are the wand of Mercury, symbolizing the carrying of traffic; the distaff, associated with Minerva, the goddess of handicrafts, significant of the industries of the country served by the railway; and the trident of Neptune, symbolizing the connection with various ports

Scottish railway coats of arms: Caledonian, Highland, Glasgow and South Western, LMS, North British, Great North of Scotland, LNER.

on the Ayrshire coast. When I first went to Scotland in 1923, the Glasgow and South Western steamships, then under LMS colours, were running on their former routes, as efficiently as ever from their original G & SWR ports at Princes Pier Greenock, at Largs and at Ardrossan, thus perpetuating the symbol of the trident of Neptune on the coat of arms of the company.

The London Midland and Scottish Railway, formed at the beginning of 1923 by amalgamation of the London and North Western, the Midland, the Lancashire and Yorkshire, the North Staffordshire, the Furness, and the three famous Scottish Companies whose insignia have already been described in this chapter, together with one or two minor associates, could well have been in a cleft stick when it came to choosing a heraldic device to cover such a diverse assembly of interest and associations. Instead the LMS adopted a very simple device including only the arms of London, the rose of England and the thistle of Scotland. When the livery of the passenger locomotives had been decided upon, and the style of the Midland Railway adopted, the coat of arms of the LMSR was put on to the cabs of the express locomotives of all vintages, as the Midland had done, and the engine numbers in huge transfer figures on the tenders. This did not work with the non-Midland constituents of the LMS, particularly on the LNWR section, which did not pair the tenders to any particular engine, and sometimes in early LMS days one saw newly repaired red tenders with black engines! Soon the numbers were removed from the tenders and put on the cab sides, replacing the coat of arms of the LMS, which thenceforward was displayed only on main-line carriages.

Lastly, in the frontispiece that I painted for the Scottish Railways book, there was that of the LNER, an amalgamation of the Great Central, Great Eastern, Great Northern, North British, North Eastern, and the Great North of Scotland, together with some smaller English local lines. Instead of some synthesis of certain constituent devices the enlarged company went to the College of Heralds and had produced for them undoubtedly the most beautiful, significant, and heraldically correct device ever associated with a British railway. The full heraldic description is:

'Argent on a Cross Gules between the first and fourth quarters a griffin sergeant Sable in the second a Rose of the second leaved and slipped proper and in third quarter a Thistle also leaved and slipped proper the Castle of Edinburgh proper between four Lions passant guardant Or And for the Crest. On a Wreath of the colour Issuant from Clouds of Steam the figure of Mercury proper.'

The motto 'Forward' was that of the former Great Central Railway. This beautiful coat of arms was reproduced in a colour-frontspiece in *The Railway Magazine* of February 1924 but no transfers were ever produced, and the only use of it made on rolling stock was when it was painted by hand on the *Flying Scotsman* locomotive, specially finished for exhibition at Wembley in 1924 and 1925.

Chapter 16
The Ocean Mail of 1904

In May 1904 there was recorded the first properly authenticated instance of a speed of 100 miles per hour on a railway. Prior to that there had been various claims to speeds even higher on certain American railways, but none of these bore close scrutiny. The first true record was that of the Great Western Railway 4-4-0 locomotive the *City of Truro* descending the Wellington bank in Somerset when the recorder, a well-established expert, clocked a speed of 102 m.p.h. with one of the Ocean Mail specials running from Plymouth to London, via Bristol. As an author with several books on train-running already to my name I felt that the fiftieth anniversary of this memorable achievement should be suitably commemorated. Just about that time, when I was Chairman of the Editorial Committee of the Westinghouse Review, the staff magazine which the management of the company sponsored for the entire work-force, I had become very friendly with the manager of the firm who did the printing of this staff magazine. He was interested in my other journalistic work and was anxious to print some of my books.

Early in the 1950s a serial article of mine on some historical work on Southern Railway locomotives in one of the technical magazines had finished. I showed Bob Stirriatt the script, and the instalments printed, and he was keen to do a book reprint. The original publishers were agreeable, and so Edward Everard's of Bristol produced the book, so handsomely done that I had no hesitation to offer them more. So they produced for me, in sumptuous form, *Fifty Years of Western Express Running*. However, before coming to the book itself and its illustrations I must tell something of the circumstances that led up to such record-breaking speeds in 1904. By the turn of the century, on the North Atlantic Ocean, rivalry between the various shipping lines was nearing a new intensity. The British ships of the Cunard and White Star lines had been well established in Liverpool for many years previously, but when the North German steamship lines based in Hamburg had been carrying British passengers, and put them ashore by tender at Plymouth, the rivalry reached a new stage. It was pointed out that by use of this new facility the journey time between New York and London could be reduced by almost a whole day. The West Country railways were very alive to this developing situation, and both the Great Western and the London and South Western Railway spent much time and money improving their facilities for handling this new traffic. At the outset there was a tacit agreement between the two companies that the London and South Western should take the passengers, all of whom were bent upon reaching London, while the Great Western took the mails.

At that time the South Western had the shortest route to London, 234 miles from the Friary station in Plymouth, skirting the northern heights of Dartmoor and then directly eastwards from Exeter via Salisbury. The Great Western was then using the original main line engineered by Brunel via Bristol, 246 miles in all. There was sound logic in the division of the traffic, because much of the mail from the North German liners was for the Midlands and North Country destinations and was unloaded from the Ocean Mail trains at Bristol. The London and South Western trains stopped once only at Templecombe, purely to change engines, whereas the Great Western stopped first of all at Exeter to detach the 4-4-0 engine used for the steeply graded South Devon line. In due course one 'City' class went through from Plymouth to Bristol. The beautiful Dean single-driver 4-2-2s were usually run from Bristol to Paddington. The 'top brass' of the locomotive department of both railways took a keen interest, particularly as the situation gradually developed into a competition to see which train, from each steamer arrival, could get its respective cargoes from Plymouth to London in the quickest time. On the South Western Dugald Drummond himself occasionally travelled in the boat train, and on one occasion had it stopped in mid-section for him to give some personal instruction to the driver. On the Great

Western Churchward summoned the locomotive inspector who had charge of the running, G H Flewellyn at Newton Abbot, and finished his instruction in these homely terms: 'withhold any attempt at a speed record until I give the word; then you can go and break your bloody neck!'

Now as to the book and its illustrations. At the very outset the then Locomotive Publishing Company gave me some splendid help, not only making their huge stock of original photographs available, but unearthing from their innermost archives some of the colour blocks from which their famous pre-1914 picture postcards had been printed. Those blocks were still in superb condition and the reproductions they gave in my own book were every bit as good as the postcards of some forty years previously. The text of the book itself covered the story of Great Western express train running in all the intervening years from 1904, illustrations *in excelsis* of all the locomotives involved. But while the reproductions made available to Edward Everard and Co. included some very historic scenes, like one of the French Compound 'Atlantics' in its original condition, a view in the newly built running shed at Old Oak Common with a variety of locomotives grouped around the nearest turntable, and above all a superb picture of *The Great Bear*, but unfortunately there was not one of a single-wheeler solo, nor any of the post-Churchward classes. Fortunately in another connection I had a very fine painting by a current friend of mine of the *King Edward VII* in British Railways colours standing up in Chippenham, which would make a splendid reproduction, and so there remained the single-wheeler.

Pondering on this I thought of course of the *City of Truro* as an alternative, seeing that she, and not a single-wheeler had topped the 100 m.p.h. mark. Actually I could not trace a single photograph of a 'City' class engine hauling one of the mail trains, though as a boy I have a clear recollection of a rather gloomy and featureless picture of 'An Ocean Mail leaving Plymouth'. The background could well have been beside some retaining wall near Millbay Docks. One of the blocks made available to me by the Locomotive Publishing Company was of a 'Flower' class outside-framed 4-4-0, and although this was in the later style of painting, and had the large copper-capped chimney it looked very like the *City of Truro* in its last pre-1914 painting. So, for a frontispiece in my new book I chose a single-wheeler. However honour was very nearly satisfied over the *City of Truro*, albeit nearly forty years later, when the 'Bradford Exchange' a firm marketing high quality porcelain plates, asked me to act as consultant to a series they were going to produce depicting famous British trains. I recommended that the GWR Ocean Mail hauled by the *City of Truro* should be one of these and I briefed their artist, my great friend Paul Gribble, to paint a picture of the record-breaking train 'doing the ton' not down the Wellington Bank but on the sea-wall at Teignmouth. His picture is beautiful and it adorns one of the cabinets in my dining room.

Reverting to the Ocean Mail of 1904, on the culminating day of the contest in speed May 9th when the record time of 3 hours 46¾ minutes was clocked up for the distance of 246½ miles, from Plymouth Millbay Docks to Paddington, including a stop of 3¾ minutes to change engines at Bristol Pylle Hill Junction, the engine for the second stage of the journey was the 4-2-2 single No. 3065 *Duke of Connaught*. Then as to a painting, there are many photographs of this notable class of locomotive including one faked-up version showing it in the so-called 'photographic grey'. At Swindon each new locomotive type, at any rate from the early 'standard gauge' days, was taken outside the Works, when given a preliminary coat of grey paint, with the lining and other embellishments in black so that the effect was very clear. When specially selected locomotives had to be photographed certain artistically minded members of the drawing office were given copies of the standard engine of a class and the name and number were painted out and the appropriate ones for the special subject to be treated substituted. Of course the official picture of the *Duke of Connaught* was no good for my purpose. Fortunately many photographs of the engines of this class, in the usual running condition have been taken; an excellent one in particular of the very engine. On the other hand this picture, taken outside the running sheds at Exeter, shows the engine in a later style of painting. The great dome was as polished and burnished as of old, but the tender has the company name in full, Great Western, on either side of the coat of arms. In 1904 the tenders were adorned with nothing more than the entwined letters on the centre panel of the side plating.

The Ocean Mail of 1904, approaching Tilehurst, Berkshire, at about 85 m.p.h. on its record run.

Then there were other hazards for an artist attempting to work up a true picture of an historic period occasion. It is true that no photographs were taken of the mail trains at speed in 1904, and contemporary reports gave no details of the loads conveyed. It was not until I managed to acquire a bound volume of the *Locomotive Magazine* for 1904 that I found an illustrated article based on information supplied by Churchward himself describing the special stowage vans that had been built for the ocean mail traffic that I appreciated the nature of the load carried on May 9th 1904. Five vans were brought up from Plymouth, and one was detached at Bristol, leaving four of these huge stowage vans to be taken on to Paddington. From the article in the *Locomotive Magazine* I learned that they were each no less than 68 ft. long, and had a tare weight of 26⅜ tons. They had three sliding doors on each side, and one of them was fitted with a guards compartment. There was no apparatus for detaching mail *en route* because no post was carried. At a later date from 1904, arrangements were made for the Bristol vehicles to be detached without stopping at Pylle Hill Junction by the usual slip-coach technique. The main part of the train then ran non-stop from Millbay Docks to Paddington. The giant stowage vans in 1904 were painted in the chocolate and cream style of the main-line passenger coaches.

The next question was where the picture should be located. Thumbing through my old volume of *The Railway Magazine* I found a very interesting, but not a very good, picture of an Ocean Mail, subsequent to the period with which I was immediately concerned, taken in the act of slipping two stowage vans off the rear of the train at Pylle Hill Junction. It was taken from the rear of the train and I could not recognize the type of engine; but whatever it was it had to pull only two vans for the rest of the journey to Paddington. For my picture I thought about several different locations. Old photographs of the Dean 'singles' at speed, on the up line, were not very frequent. I thought of the woodland stretch just after St Annes park where the engine first worked up speed. Then there was the eastern end of Box Tunnel, where there was an attractive 'F Moore' coloured postcard, and then, of course, there was Sonning Cutting. But I discarded all these, and having a good photograph of a Dean 'single' at speed with an up Worcester express near Hayes, with nothing of background to speak of, I implanted it into one of my own photographs on the picturesque stretch of line west of Tilehurst where the speed of the Ocean Mail of 9 May 1904 was about 82 m.p.h.

Bob Stirratt was delighted with the picture, and the reproduction turned out well and made a handsome frontispiece to the book. With the 'F Moore' paintings on the blocks loaned by the Locomotive Publishing Company I was certainly in some strong competition, and there was also Welch's fine picture of the *King Edward VII* near the end of the book. The Ocean Mail and the *KEVII* came back to me after publication but the blocks of the F Moore pictures, alas, went back to the publishers. Not many years later, the Locomotive Publishing Company were absorbed into the Ian Allan Group, and they in due course approached me to update the book and republished it as *Sixty Years of Western Express Running.* Several new chapters were added to bring the story fully up to date and when it was re-published in 1974 it ran to more than 400 pages with the gradient profiles added, as in the first edition. Ian Allan's provided many additional photographs but, as to colour, things were not very happy. I was told that the colour blocks we had used in the first edition, and which by the results Everard's achieved with them seemed in first-class condition, were not available. I had the original painting of the *King Edward VII* and of the Ocean Mail on my walls, and I took the pictures out of the frames and sent them to Ian Allan's I heard nothing more until the new edition actually appeared.

That new edition, which should have been another of my top favourites was in many ways a disappointment. The black and white photographs, very well reproduced it is true, were massed in three solid blocks instead of being spread through the text appropriate to the subject matter under discussion. But then the colour – ! A four sheet 'wodge' was all that was included. Two sheets of this had the paintings I had already sent, and the other two were from other contributors. The reproduction on these two was ghastly – there is no other word for it. The Welch painting of the *King Edward VII* was better, though not nearly as good as Edward Everard's rendered it in the first edition. My own picture of the Ocean Mail was the best reproduction of all four, though covering an entire page, and with the colour rendering inclined to be garish it did not please me much. The only saving grace was that those awful insertions were set on pages facing each other and not adjacent to either Welch's picture or my own. I am sorry to finish this piece about the Ocean Mail on something of a sour note, but the disappointment I felt at the time was intense.

Chapter 17

South Devon Cliffs – Looking towards the Parson and Clerk

At the end of April 1924 I left home for London for what was hoped would be the last term in my three-year course in engineering training at Imperial College, at the conclusion of which I hoped to emerge as an Associate of the City and Guilds Institute and a Bachelor of Science in Engineering. Even before I left home my father, confident in my success in the crucial examinations, was making plans in two directions. Seeing that if I graduated in the early summer that I should be no more than 19 years of age he considered that no one would give me anything of a job, and that he was arranging to give me an extra years at college as a post-graduate student for any advanced course of training that I fancied. Furthermore, in celebration of my success in the term-end examinations, so it was hoped (!!), the annual holiday for the family should be in West Cornwall. This was a delightful prospect, because I should have once again the three-months college vacation and be able to spend the month of my father's annual leave from the bank with them.

Term-end at College came and went and I returned to Barrow anxiously to await the verdict. Almost the first news I had, indeed I recall it was the very first, came from the residents in the Toc H Mark in Queens Gate Gardens, South Kensington, where I had lived throughout my three years at Imperial College. It was a telegram couched in the style of Sir W S Gilbert in 'HMS Pinafore', suitable parodied thus:

116

'Examiners have said it,
And it's greatly to his credit
He becomes a B.Sc!'

I rode off to Newby Bridge on my bicycle with a high heart that day,
meanwhile preparations continued for our trip to Penzance. In mid-
August we travelled down on 'The Cornish Riviera Express', and
lunched in style in the restaurant car. After passing Exeter I made a
break in my train-timing activities and joined my sister and another
girl friend in the corridor to see something of the coast stretch of the
line, west of Starcross. But unfortunately the fine weather in which
we had left London had turned sour as we had come westwards and
before we had passed Taunton it was raining. In such conditions the
coastal stretch looked depressing in the extreme, with little colour
on the high red cliffs between Dawlish and Teignmouth.

The weather was a complete contrast when we returned a month
later; brilliant sunshine, enticing me to go there at the earliest opportunity to take railway photographs beneath those glorious red
cliffs, even though the speed of the trains was usually at least 50
m.p.h. beside that delightful sea wall that extended almost to the
Parson's tunnel. But I have unfortunately an unpleasant memory of
that ride on the up Cornish Riviera Express that almost took the
glitter from the fine performance of the engine *Malvern Abbey* which
took us through from Plymouth to Paddington. At that young age I
had not become so adept in keeping the engine grit from my eyes
when looking out of train windows; and I arrived at Paddington with
a sizeable piece in my right eye, at any rate it felt like that! We were
staying at the Euston Hotel that night and repeated washings of my
eye failed to dislodge the particle. It was worse next morning, and my
mother and sister together rendered first aid unavailingly. We travelled north by the summer service 11.25 a.m., a curious train that
made a non-stop run from Rugby to Wigan and then having changed
engines went on non-stop to Lancaster. The traffic operating was
appalling, because, delayed by signals, we lost almost half an hour on
the run to Lancaster. By that time my eye was getting inflamed, and
although the doctor was notified as soon as we got home he was not
able to come till the following morning. The result of my ride on the

Cornish Riviera Express was a shade over that eye for the next few days!

Next summer the family went to Paignton, but although I took my bicycle with me and did a lot of riding when it came to the Teignmouth sea-wall and the taking of many railway photographs I went by the local train service. The weather was glorious, so I got to work early one morning and with plenty of films had my fill of 'Saint' and 'Star' class 4-6-0s. In 1925 the 'Castles' were few and far between. Swindon Works had only just commenced delivery of the second batch of those famous engines. All of the first ten were first stationed at Old Oak Common, and the first two to be shedded elsewhere, in this case at Laira, were *Berkeley Castle* and *Builth Castle*, which I saw in due course on this particular holiday. At that time Bristol had no four cylinder engines, and 'Saints' were much in evidence on the West to North trains. On the first day on which I was on the sea wall both the up and down Cornish Riviera Expresses were hauled by 'Stars' respectively *King Edward* and *Queen Adelaide*. The 'King' class proper were not even contemplated in 1925. After photographing the *Queen Adelaide* I walked up the Smugglers Lane footpath to the main road from Teignmouth towards Dawlish, to see if there was any access to the line beyond the Parsons Tunnel.

In 1990, sixty-five years after my first explorations in the district – *sixty-five years* mark you! – a charming little paperback, entitled *Rails along the Sea Wall* was published by a firm in Sheffield, of all places. It included a host of recent photographs, many of them in colour, but also an addendum, a series of carefully drawn sketch-maps, showing all the footpaths giving access to the line, from Dawlish Warren to Teignmouth Eastcliff. In my own primeval explorations it did not take me a very long walk on that main road to find a footpath leading coastways again, and it brought me to that once hazardous stretch of line where the one-time single-tracked broad gauge railway was completely blocked by a great landslip, and which I had seen illustrated by a famous drawing of early days on the line, and which is noted on the railway by the so-called Breeches Rock. Working now from the landward side of the railway I was in time to photograph the Penzance–Wolverhampton express, going powerfully behind the *Bride of Lammermoor*, and giving a fine smoke effect rarely seen on this part of the GWR where the gradients are non-existent and the steaming is usually easy. The train had just emerged from the 1921 eastward extension of the Parsons Tunnel, built to provide additional shelter from the danger of falling rocks.

Looking Eastwards the stark, well-nigh vertical wall of red sandstone cliff made an impressive entrance to the next tunnel, the 'Clerks', only 58 yards long. The only disadvantage in photographing on the stretch of line is the absence of any signals. The Dawlish up distant is nearer to the station. Very soon there was a rumble eastwards and I was ready to 'cop' the newly commissioned *Builth Castle* at the head of a lengthy West of England express emerging from the Clerks tunnel. Armed with a walking permit I was tempted to go through the short tunnel, but the short space before the even shorter Phillot tunnel was not photogenic so I went through the 49 yard bore, and then found Coryton tunnel ahead of me – 227 yards long, straight, with a ready-made walkway to the right of the permanent way. On sober reflection, all these years after the event, I can see that the decision to go through the tunnel was the most foolhardy act of my life: until then I was quite alone, no trains had passed, since I had photographed *Builth Castle*, I had not seen any surface men, and then I went into the blackness of the tunnel. The exit end was quite clear. There was no smoke hanging about, just darkness and I must have panicked and began to run. Suddenly I tripped over a heap of old timber and fell prostrated in the darkness. Mercifully I was unhurt, though badly shaken, but I could easily have fallen awkwardly, and being injured fallen across one of the running rails, and that might have been the end of O.S.N.

I picked myself up, *walked* very gingerly to the far end of the tunnel, and then, as if nothing had happened, mingled with the holidaymakers enjoying themselves on Coryton Beach, where they had presumably reached by boat. There was no access from the cliffs. I do not recall how I ever got back to Teignmouth sea wall. I must have braved the 227 yard tunnel again, but not running this time. Fortunately my clothes were undamaged in the fall and I did not tell either of my parents, or my sister of my adventure in the Coryton Tunnel. It was some time before I had to go, and supervise maintenance work in the tunnels and then naturally I had plenty of company and proper lighting! But I shall always look wistfully through that paperback *Rails along the Sea Wall* and wonder if any of the modern readers had a self-inflicted nightmare like mine.

After the year 1926, for the remainder of the time my father was manager of Barclay's Bank in Barrow-in-Furness, my parents did not visit South Devon again for their annual holiday. They went instead to the Highlands of Scotland, and after my father had retired they certainly could not afford to spend a month away, as previously. My own railway interests were getting more widespread, and so it was not until the Second World War ended, and my young family had reached 'the bucket and spade' era that Olivia and I thought again of South Devon. The London Office of Westinghouse had not been returned to their pre-war accommodation at Kings Cross. We were just installed in a huge Georgian house in Sion Hill in Bath, and we thought of Devon as an easily and cheaply reached 'bucket and spade' holiday. Furthermore, we were fortunate to find a comfortable, relatively cheap boarding house on the sea front at Teignmouth. The sands were ready at hand, and for me, needless to say, there was the nearby sea wall with the Great Western main line running along it! I photographed all sorts and conditions of trains during the several holidays we had there, but there was another interest too arising out of the important commission I had received from Nelsons to write a book on Scottish Railways.

Their editorial department were insistent that there should be an abundance of colour plates, and having been shown some of my earlier efforts they promptly commissioned me to paint some of the pictures. This gave me a renewed interest in water-colour painting, and on one of those holiday visits to Teignmouth I took some sketch blocks and one of my less used paint boxes. I had always kept the rather posh outfit I used for my earlier work, but this time, realizing that some of my colour sketches would have to be done in somewhat alfresco conditions, I took an outfit that had been used by my children, in their very young days. So, on one very fine Sunday morning when there were few trains to spot, the family were happily established on the beach very close to our hotel and I got out a sketch block and began to sketch out the very attractive red cliffs through which the railway tunnelled at the Parson and Clerk rocks. The

The red cliffs of South Devon, sketched from the beach of Teignmouth.

sketch was quickly done, and with the children busily engaged in the usual sea-beach activities I was able to get my water-colours out and start a proper picture. Inevitably, passers-by looked over my shoulder and made remarks that were either facetious or non-committal, when suddenly all was panic stations!

My son, who could not have been more than six or seven years old at that time was stung by a wasp. My daughter, three years older, howled in sympathy and Olivia gave some impromptu first aid. But it appeared to be a bad sting, and we gathered up some of our most immediate effects and took them just across the road to where our rooms were. The crisis was however soon over and I went across to the beach to gather up the rest of our things which had been left on the two deck chairs where Olivia and I had been sitting before 'the balloon went up'. Most of it was undisturbed, including my water-colour sketch of the red cliffs, but of my paint-box, my brushes and the little beaker in which I had some fresh water for painting there was not a trace! I cannot remember now if I had finished the picture, and at the time Olivia and I regarded the loss of that cheap paint-box as 'one of those things', as the saying then went. Whether the picture was actually finished *in situ*, or in my own home at Bath does not matter now. Eventually we had it framed and it now hangs on one of the walls in my present home.

Rails along the Sea Wall; what memories that little paperback brings to me. The first time I ever rode on a locomotive that way was in somewhat unusual circumstances. The war was still on and I had been commissioned by an American publisher to write something of how the British railways, not of course then nationalized, were coping with the war conditions. I was very much involved in war work of my own professional duties, but I was able to spare a single day and the GWR gave me an engine pass to ride the morning West to North express from Newton Abbot through to Shrewsbury, which was worked by one engine. I went down by an evening train, heavily blacked out of course, and the next morning I joined the crew on a resplendent *Usk Castle*. The train stopped at Teignmouth and Dawlish and the locomotive inspector, who was riding with us, ushered me across from the fireman's corner of the cab, where I had positioned myself, to the seaward side. That day it was all calm, but in the earlier days of the war, lone aerial raiders had attacked Teignmouth and Newton Aboot, and in this latter case done some damage to railway property and rolling stock. But in October 1944 when my own journey was made the tide of battle was happily flowing inexorably towards the Rhine!

I often recall another footplate ride when the weather conditions were far less favourable. I had an engine pass to travel on the morning express from the West of England to Birmingham and Wolverhampton, and the Cornish part of the train, which I joined at Plymouth, then made a non-stop run through to Exeter. We had one of the earlier 4-6-0s, of the 'Star' class, for this part of the journey, the *Princess Charlotte* in fact, and in her rather scanty cab I became distinctly wet even before we got to the sea wall. Once out of the cutting past Teignmouth we took the full force of the storm. At high tide the waves were coming right over the wall and crashing on to the railway, and we on the exposed footplate got more than one ducking from the spray before we reached the shelter of the tunnels. Incidentally I was much intrigued in the paperback to see the one excrescence in the sea wall between Teignmouth and the Parson rock named as 'Sprey Point'. I was evidently not a misprint for it was repeated several times in the text, and also in the caption to one of the illustrations. In all our various visits to Teignmouth I never recall hearing the name used. 'Spray' seems much more appropriate!

My later excursions, on the Western Region, as it became, to collect data for some of my literary work, were usually arranged to coincide with our annual visits to Teignmouth and then if the times were convenient the family were often assembled on the sea wall to wave me on my way. I shall always remember one occasion when I had a pass to ride the down Cornish Riviera Express on a Saturday morning in high summer. The train itself was booked to run from Paddington to Truro without any stops. I had travelled up to London on the previous afternoon and was aware of the operational procedure whereby the London engine was detached at Newton Abbot and replaced by two smaller engines for the run, not stopping at Plymouth, into Cornwall. On this particular occasion we had caught up with the procession of earlier trains and we were being much delayed by the adverse signals along the coastal stretch. My family and friends were there to see us go through from Sprey Point to Teignmouth, and we were going so slowly that I was to shout a greeting from the footplate of our 'King' class engine!

Chapter 18

Portree – Looking south towards Glamaig

The first time I ever saw the great mountains of Skye, albeit from afar, was in 1927 when, with my father, mother and young sister, we made a railway trip from Inverness to the Kyle of Lochalsh. It was a very fine day in early September, and while the maps that I had with me did not extend to the Western Highlands, and I was not able to identify the mountains ranged across the sea from the foreshore at the Kyle, the sight of them in the distance was enough to strengthen a resolve to go over to Skye at the first opportunity that came my way. On the other hand my spare-time interests at that time were as much with railways as with mountain scenery, and having had a fair share of both in two successive visits to the region of Inverness, in 1927 and 1928, our family holidays were directed elsewhere in the remaining two years of my father's time as a bank manager in Barrow-in-Furness. It was not until the late summer of 1932 that I went to Inverness again, on my own this time, on a round tour that I hoped would provide me with much interesting data in locomotive running, railway photography, and some fine mountain scenery. I went, after a preliminary weekend in Perth, from Inverness on the morning train to the Kyle of Lochalsh, and then on the Macbrayne mail steamer to Portree, an old single-funnelled paddle-boat.

The weather was far different from that we had enjoyed on our first visit to the Kyle. Although wet and stormy there were intervals of marvellously clear skies, which even with the monochrome film that I was then using brought promise of some spectacular pictures, or so I thought. I have been looking through the album that contains the photographs I took on that holiday, particularly those I took from the mail boat on the journey from Kyle to Portree, and I must say some of them, especially one, could be described as spectacular, not exactly idyllic – great mountains sheathed in rain, while the immediate waterway in which we were making a stormy way was in sunshine! It had cleared up when we reached Portree, with the late afternoon sunshine making the sweep of the little bay look delightful. There was a much larger steamer at the jetty, so the mail boat had to berth alongside of her, and passengers, luggage, cargo and mails had to be humped across the deck of the other steamer to reach the jetty. I photographed the two ships when I reached the shore but at this distance in time I cannot remember the name or affiliation of the ship. Our mail-boat was the *Fusilier*. I cannot recall how I spent my first evening in Portree having got over the incredibly cramped rooms of the cottage in which I was booked for the best part of a week.

The following morning broke beautifully fine, and having collected some rations for the day I caught the bus going south, intending to alight at the Sligachan Inn and walk my way up the glen of the same name within ideal photographic range of the most spectacular of the Cuillins, Sgurr nan Gillean. But in some ten miles of bumpy moorland road, although Class A on the Ordnance Survey map, the skies had clouded over, and another walker who was apparently heading the same way, and who proved pleasant company, feared we should get heavy rain by afternoon. As soon as we had left the bus and had started walking up the glen I was soon taking photographs of Sgurr nan Gillean, but my companion suggested that I should leave plenty of exposures for 'the other side' as he called it. I should explain we were both heading for the path that led over the rocky heights to west of the glen from which there was a sight of that most forbidding of water, Loch Coruisk. Once on the ridge I looked down on one of the most desolate sights I ever remember. The rain clouds were clustering on the higher slopes. I remembered the rather grim painting of Loch Coruisk in one of my books, but on this day it looked infinitively worse – there was not a vestige of colour in the scene. I photographed the wee lochan that we passed on the way down, that the Ordnance Survey map names as Loch a'Choire Rhabheidich, but my pictures, also of Loch Coruisk itself, although in monochrome, might have been taken in colour for all the tints they could show.

Before even I took my photographs the rain was sweeping across from the west, and my companion and I had a very wet walk over the seven miles back to the shelter of the Sligachan Inn. I was wet through because the raincoat I had on was not waterproofed against such a downpour as this! Fortunately the cottagers with whom I was lodged were well used to their visitors getting back from their excursions in this kind of state, and once I had stripped off, and changed, my wet clothes were gathered up and returned dry ready for the next day's adventure. I spent the next day quietly, however, walking around Portree and sketching from my bedroom window the picturesque row of cottages on the road leading to the pier. I had not got any water-colours with me on this trip, nor any proper drawing paper, but I made a rough sketch on one of the pages of the large notebook I always carried for train-timing activities. From my Ordnance Survey Map I learned that the twin-crested mountain I could see from this viewpoint was Glamaig, not far from the Sligachan Inn where I had sheltered on the previous afternoon. There were no vessels at the little jetty when I made my first sketch, but when the *Fusilier* arrived back from her daily visit to Kyle of Lochalsh and Mallaig I added her to my drawing.

It was many months later before I took up the sketch I had made in my train-running log book to paint the picture in water-colour. By that time I had processed the many photographs I had taken on that fortnight's trip to Scotland, and they had brought back many memories of the holiday. I had taken a photograph from the bedroom window of that cottage in Portree, from almost the same viewpoint as my first sketch was made, and that photograph brought home more clearly than anything else the vivid contrasts of the scenery I had enjoyed in that brief stay in Skye. In addition to that very damp excursion to see Loch Coruisk I had made another, with considerably better weather, to the far north of the district of Trotternish, and another by the coastal road southwards from Portree that led to the entrance to Loch Sligachan, a sea-loch that winds inland between the heights of Glamaig. From my map I noted that there was no road at the loch side, only a footpath, but recalling what I experienced going over to see Loch Coruisk I was prepared for the worst.

When I was in Kyle of Lochalsh in 1928 I had bought Canon MacCulloch's lovely book *The Misty Isle of Skye*, and my desire to see more of the island than a brief glimpse across the waterway, as well as from the train from Inverness, was enhanced. After a gap of sixty years I cannot remember how I came to make the trip round the peninsular of Trotternish, whether it was by a touring bus or whether it was by some means of hired transport. But the photographs I secured, which are still in a state of good preservation today, show that I had plenty of time to seek out the most advantageous view-points for taking some of the interesting places on the way. Reading once again *The Misty Isle of Skye* I see that I made the circuit of the peninsular of Trotternish in the reverse way to that followed by the author of this fascinating book but he, for a time, was resident, as the Rector of St Columba's Church in Portree, whereas I was only on a week's holiday visit. Looking through my much treasured photographs I am surprised to see how much of the peninsular I covered on that one day. My route evidently made for the shores of Loch Snizort, for the first of my photographs was not until we had passed Uig Bay. Then, apparently, I got busy in earnest.

Skye is essentially Macleod country, through the continued residence of Macleod of Macleod at Dunvegan Castle. I am ashamed to say I never found time to visit Dunvegan though I cherish the friendship of another Macleod who was a senior locomotive engineer on the Southern Railway of England, and who was a Member of the Clan Macleod 'Parliament' which meets from time to time at Dunvegan Castle under the presidency of Macleod of Macleod. Trotternish however is ancient Macdonald territory though the links with the past are those of ancient memorials rather than living personalities. In my own time, north of Uig Bay, I was taken to see a monument to one of the greatest romances in British history. Canon MacCulloch writes that, to the lover of the romantic, few places in this solitary land could give greater pleasure. He names it as the Reileag Mhoir Chlonin Dounill, the burial place of the Macdonalds of the Isles, and here, he adds, lies the dust of her whose name is best known of all her clan, Flora Macdonald. How she shielded 'Bonnie Prince Charlie' when he was on the run after the Battle of Culloden Moor is well known, in general terms, but the details are not so well known. When she died, at Kingsburgh, Skye, she was buried in one of the sheets the Prince slept in when he was in her care in the family home.

I was taken to see the great Iona cross and the massive slab of granite that covers her grave, and on the slab is inscribed this:

FLORA MACDONALD
Born at Milton South Uist 1722
Died at Kingsburgh Skye, March 1790

So, she lived for 44 years after saving the Prince from the Hanoverian Troops. This great white cross, which I photographed, is visible far out to sea, and is exposed to the fury of the wild winter storms. When I was there I noted that it had been strengthened by some metallic reinforcements.

Our next stop was at Duntulm, where the narrow coast road turns abruptly east across the uppermost part of Trotternish. For centuries the castle here was the home of the Chief of the Macdonald of the Isles, but now it is only a fragment of a ruin. It stands on a lofty mound, and in days gone by its windows looked sheer into the sea. MacCulloch says that seawards it was unapproachable, and from the land side could scarcely have been less so. I photographed the two isolated columns, all that remains of the ancient keep, from some distance, to give the impression that I felt of the solitude of the place, and I walked right up to the ruin and took more pictures through the columns of the sea below. The results were purely documentary – nothing to paint in water-colours. I was told that the views across the sea of The Little Minch to the Outer Hebrides could be very fine, but on the day I was there the skies were overcast, and in fact the whole ride up the western side of Trotternish seemed rather devoid of interest, except for the Flora Macdonald cross and the few remains of Duntulm Castle.

The road winds due east across the top of the peninsular and soon there was a broad view over to the mainland coast with the high

O.S NOCK 1933

Portree, Isle of Skye: the harbour sketched from my bedroom window, looking south towards Glamaig.

mountains of Torridon showing but vaguely in the rather misty atmosphere of this early September day. Soon my attention was drawn to the striking formations of the steep rocky face of the northerly height in the chain that extends from Portree, as it were a continuous spine, throughout the length of Trotternish. From my map I learned it is named Meall na Snirdmach. However, it is not the summit of the mountain, albeit rising to 1779 feet above sea level, that claims attention at this stage, but the black cliffs of the Quiraing, as the remarkable amphitheatre of basaltic rock that forms the eastern façade of the mountain range is known. Canon MacCulloch, who had plenty of opportunity for exploring in his time of residence at Portree, has a vivid description of the details of this rocky wilderness, extending to nearly two enthralling pages of his book, but I had to be content with a sight of it from the main road and the photographs I secured really give no idea of the astonishing nature of the place. On this grey day when even I with my long-sighted vision (which incidentally, despite having added sixty years to my life since that day in Skye is as good as ever; no need for spectacles except for close reading) I could not make out the 'bewildering series of precipices and pinnacles' that Canon MacCulloch so vividly describes. Several miles further on we stopped for a backward look at it, but the photograph I took gives not the slightest impression of the place.

We stopped again at the Kilt Rock for me to take a photograph of the miniature cascade that tumbles down the vertical cliff face straight into the sea, and then on to a first sight of The Storr. This massive-looking mountain is the highest point in the range stretching northwards from Portree to the Quiraing, rising to 2358 feet. Its northern aspect is the least spectacular, although even from there, the isolated pinnacle of the Old Man of Storr can be descried rising above one of the upper ridges. I was told that the actual approach to the Old Man is strewn with boulders and rocks, making a more northerly, and lesser, version of the wildest regions of the Cuillins, with the Old Man himself a huge pillar, 150 ft. high, standing apart from the rest. My first photograph taken from the northern side, like those of the Quiraing gives not the slightest impression of the place, and after we had passed abreast of the Old Man those driving me were evidently anxious to get back to Portree, before the rain which had been threatening all day finally closed in on us. Two days later, my last day on Skye, I walked out the three miles on the north road from Portree as far as Loch Fada, and got some reasonably satisfactory, albeit rather distant, views of The Storr.

On the previous day when the weather was reasonably fine I walked some ten or twelve miles by the coastal road south from Portree until it ended in a mere footpath by the side of the sea-loch Sligachan with the towering mass of Glamaig just across the water. The coastal road gave me a constant picture of the southern end of the small island of Raasay no more than two miles across the water, and while I was watching, the daily mail-steamer from the Kyle came chugging along with her paddle-wheels thrusting purposefully into the breezy water. From this distance I could see that she carried many more passengers than when I had come. But this was a Saturday, and when I had caught the late afternoon bus from the Sligachan Inn back to Portree, I found that in the cottages by the quay-side there was a whole contingent of hikers, judging from their rather loud voices from the industrial districts of West Yorkshire. The rest of my walk on the muddy footpath along Loch Sligachan was uneventful. Glamaig at close quarters was just mighty big, without any of the spires, pinnacles, and precipices of the Cuillins, now so relatively near.

Back in my quayside lodgings in Portree I felt that the rough pencil sketch I had previously made would satisfy my impressions of those five days in Skye. I had rarely seen the marvellous colours of the sea and skies so vividly described as in Canon MacCulloch's book, and when I came to paint the scene I had sketched, the red funnel of the MacBrayne paddle-steamer at the jetty was the only real splash of the colour in the scene. This is one of the few pictures I painted that my father did not have framed. It was put into a portfolio, and there it remained for upwards of forty years until it was extracted in the present context.

Chapter 19

Denthead Viaduct – a Southbound Midland express crossing

When in December 1939, of all unlikely dates, George Lake in his usual enterprising spirit introduced a new monthly magazine named *Railways*, some photographers who had been rather shy of offering their work to the long-established organs of the railway press went in, with some very interesting results. One of these was a man named Charles Doncaster who had been to a boarding school in Reading in the last years of the broad gauge on the Great Western. With the rather primitive equipment then available he took many remarkably successful photographs of Great Western trains and engines and from his wartime home, that I gathered was in Sheffield, he contributed a fascinating series of articles on the railway scene around Reading in the 1890s. As one who had come to live at Reading in 1905 we soon got into correspondence, and I then discovered that he was then Chairman of a family steel-making firm, Daniel Doncaster and Co., operating in the original premises in Sheffield. Naturally he had extended his photographic activities to other railways than the Great Western, and the pen-friendship developed.

Then during the grimmest years of the Second World War, an associated company of Westinghouse, based in Sheffield, who looked after our interests in the coal-mining business received an enquiry from a colliery on the North-east coast. Our Sheffield agents did not seem to make head or tail of what was needed, except that it was extremely urgent! Soon it was decided that the colliery engineer and I should meet in Sheffield. This was easier said than done in wartime, but our agents assured me that they would fix up some hotel accommodation for the several nights that it was expected I would need to be away. Sheffield! The business meetings would not extend to evening entertainment, and my first evening in the rather drab little boarding house, which was all our agents could find at such short notice, was depressing in the extreme. Then I suddenly thought of Charles Doncaster. I found his name in the telephone directory and rang him up at an address in a village named Bradfield. I did not know where it was and I had no map to consult. He greeted me cordially and invited me to his home next evening. At that stage in the war there were no such things as cars for purely commuter runs between home and place of business, even for directors of companies busily engaged on urgent war production, so our rendezvous on the following evening was at the bus station.

Our route followed the course of the River Loxley almost due west of the City into the foothills of the Derbyshire Peak District. Sheffield itself is only about fifteen miles from The Peak itself, and in the Loxley valley there are several small lakes that have been made into reservoirs for augmenting the water supplies of the City of Sheffield. The war itself had reached a fairly advanced stage by then, though not to the point of the D-Day landings. But the mighty power of the British Bomber Command was being ceaselessly and relentlessly used to destroy strategic targets in enemy-held territory, and not long before I went to Sheffield we had all heard of the devastating raid that had resulted in the destruction of the Mohne Dam. At home the most stringent precautions were taken in case of any reprisals of a like kind against our own hydro-electric installations, and one case was the protection of the reservoirs in the Loxley Valley, damage to which would cause chaos in Sheffield. I was thrilled to see the immense balloon barrage erected across the approach to the so-called Damflask reservoirs, beside which our bus took us to Bradfield village, where Charles Doncaster lived in his widowhood. Once inside his severely blacked-out home however the talk was far removed from current wartime conditions.

From his contributions to the magazine *Railways*, and the numerous excellent photographs reproduced therein I had gathered the impression that my host that evening was also a dedicated Midland enthusiast. All his photographs and his writings so far had been of far bygone years, and it was not until I met him personally that I realized his interests were very far from being confined to the turn of the century, as far as locomotives and train workings were concerned. He must have been some twenty years senior to me in age, but his enthusiasm seemed as keen as ever. He presented me with a beautiful photograph of the southbound, 'Silver Jubilee', streamlined express of the LNER which I subsequently painted for a colour plate in one of my later books, and which forms the subject of the final chapter in this present book. From the Midland Railway of old our talk that night ranged into Scotland, and the Scottish locomotives he had photographed in and around Carlisle. Then we digressed to talk of my own early days at Giggleswick School and my recollections of the southern end of the Settle and Carlisle line in the years 1916 to 1921 when I was a boarder there.

While by the outbreak of the Second World War I had travelled over the Settle and Carlisle line many times, though not yet on the footplate, I had not yet had any opportunity of seeing the line from the outside, as it were, apart from the few miles north of Settle itself which were within reach in a half-day's holiday push-bike ride from school. Charles Doncaster, in his motoring days before the Second World War, knew the country well, evidently loved it all, and showed me many photographs, scenic as well as railways, that excited my imagination. It was the first time I had seen true pictures of the line and its marvellous viaducts, tunnel entrances and mountain scenery; I fear my interest carried me so far away that night as to ask for prints of some of the most intriguing pictures – very naughty no doubt seeing how photographic material was in short supply at the time. But he turned up trumps and in due course sent me a handsome selection of the pictures in which I was particularly interested.

One of these was a shot of Denthead Viaduct. He had photographed it from a high-level viewpoint on the very minor way that leads up from the valley of the River Dee towards Newby Head to the junction with the road from Ingleton to Hawes which the Settle and Carlisle main line crosses at Ribblehead. It was a marvellous viewpoint, looking down across the line of the railway, to a majestic panorama of Pennine hill country, taking in Rise Hill heaving up to its summit point in Ayen Gill Pike, 1825 ft. above sea level, and separating the valley of Dee from that of Garsdale. At Denthead Viaduct the railway has only just emerged from the fearsome Blea Moor Tunnel. After the arduous ascent of The Long Drag, fifteen miles of it with all but a few hundred yards or so inclined at 1 in 100, the line is more or less level over the next eight miles of rugged country over which the track is carried on high embankments, deep cuttings, and the tunnel is indeed dead level. It is here that the Midland Railway laid in water troughs to enable non-stop running over the 113 miles between Leeds and Carlisle to be made without the use of the heavy bogie tenders that had been introduced at the end of the 19th century.

In the photograph Charles Doncaster took, on the skyline, beyond the massive shoulder of Rise Hill, can be seen a still greater mountain mass. This was Baugh Fell, humped above Garsdale, through which the Clough River runs westward. The highest point of Baugh Fell is 2216 ft. above sea level, not quite equal to those of the heights that flank 'The Long Drag', Whernside, Ingleborough and Pen-y-ghent, but in its great bulk it is in some ways the giant of them all. No more than its profile could be seen in Doncaster's photograph, above the intervening Rise Hill. The line was conceived and planned as a major express route throughout. Its services would be highly competitive with the well-established East and West Coast routes from London to Scotland and in consequence the remit set before the construction engineers in such difficult country was severe. How skilfully they did their work can be gauged from the fact that when the structures, the lofty embankments and the deep cuttings had settled down, after about 15 to 20 years of regular running, there was no need to impose a single restriction in speed, beyond those put on temporarily while routine maintenance work was in progress. Maximum speeds up to 90 m.p.h. could be safely run on the descending sections of line. The line had been opened for express passenger traffic in 1876 and by the end of the century the line was ready for the highest speeds that then could be run.

The construction of Denthead Viaduct marked the terminating point of No. 1 contract. This, including the Long Drag up from Settle Junction, involved the tremendous jobs of Ribblehead Viaduct

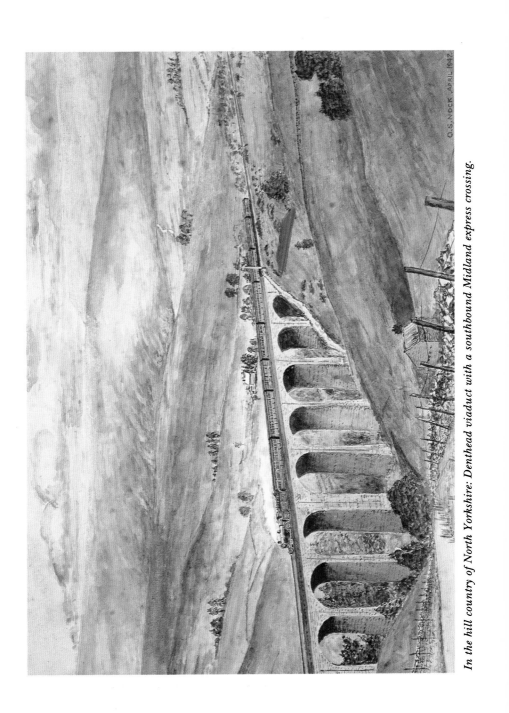

In the hill country of North Yorkshire: Denthead viaduct with a southbound Midland express crossing.

and Blea Moor tunnel, and by comparison with these Denthead was a straightforward job. Not that there was variation in the quality of the work performed. There are ten arches and the openings are 45 ft. across. The centre post was made much wider as a safeguard against the danger of the other slenderer piers collapsing through damage. In this event the existence of a more massive central pier might prevent the whole viaduct collapsing. Construction is of blue limestone, with brick arch rings. The same form of construction was used by the contractor in the Blea Moor Viaduct. It is interesting that in the very next viaduct on the line, Arten Gill, only 1¼ miles further north, which came within No. 2 contract, the constructor, although keeping the appearance of the viaduct the same, built it entirely of stone, quarried locally, known as Dent marble, actually a dark grey limestone with white fossils. At long range Arten Gill was more impressive than Denthead. It has eleven arches and they had a maximum height of 117 ft. above the valley floor as against 100 ft. at Denthead. But there was no road where one could drive a car beneath Arten Gill Viaduct, and Doncaster never seems to have indulged in a pedestrian scramble up the heathery slopes of Great Knoutberry Hill which rises to 2200 ft. east of the railway.

As soon as I received his print of Denthead Viaduct I determined to paint the scene. The photograph was of course in monochrome but I had plenty of experience of the vagaries of wind and weather, storm and calm shining, in my five years at Giggleswick to supply all the authentic touches; the train was the problem. Express passenger trains on the Settle and Carlisle line were not all that frequent, even in the most competitive days of the Midland Railway. Doncaster's photograph shows a northbound mixed goods hauled by a humdrum Class 4 0-6-0 goods engine, heading away from the camera. This would certainly not do for me. Something coming the other way would seem more appropriate. Knowing something of the operating problems of that mountainous stretch of line I thought at first of a double-header, but then I recalled that the southbound expresses that needed pilot assistance from Carlisle almost always stopped at Ais Gill to detach the leading engine, and I remembered one particular occasion when I was travelling south from Edinburgh when our train engine continued unassisted from Ais Gill with a load of 13 bogie coaches. Certainly then there were plenty of double-headers going north across Denthead Viaduct, because trains that were heavy enough to need assistance from Hellifield took their pilots forward and detached them at Ais Gill summit.

I toyed with the idea of having a northbound double-header in my picture. But the trouble was no railway photographer of any reputation, in those days, positioned himself to take a rearward view of the locomotives, except on some special assignment, and good pictures were virtually non-existent. So I had to rely on a conventional viewpoint. Next was the question what locomotive I should include. Even up to the outbreak of the Second World War the choice was limitless. The viaduct and the moorland scenery in the background had not changed since the line was built in 1876. Midland express engines were green at that time, and one choice could have been of a Kirtley 2-4-0. Then there was the early 'red' era when the Derby maintained engines had the letters M R on their tenders and their numbers in relatively small but highly polished brass figures on their cab sides. On the institution of the Train Control system every engine on the line, passenger, goods, shunting alike, had the numbers painted in huge letters on the tenders or on the side tanks of tank engines. This was all very well in the palmy days before the First World War, but in the early LMS days, when increased locomotive utilization became a watchword, engines became separated from their tenders, and on the occasion of my heavy load trip previously mentioned the Midland compound No. 1070 was running with a tender carrying in huge numerals 1108!

Then, following the grouping of the railways there came the interchange trials when certain London and North Western express locomotives were tested between Leeds and Carlisle – black engines instead of Midland red. A few years later when more powerful engines had been introduced on to the West Coast route from Euston some locomotives, of the 'Claughton' class, were transferred to the Midland Division. Their power rating was Class 5, as against Class '4' for the Midland compounds. Thus the ex-LNWR engines could take heavier loads, and this reduced the amount of double-heading that was needed with heavy trains over the Settle and Carlisle line. They were painted red at that time and the cleaners at the running sheds of Leeds and Carlisle kept them always very smart. So what I had to choose from was a pageant of fifty years or more, ranging from the green Kirtley outside framed 2-4-0s to the red 'Claughtons' transferred from the former LNW line. The choice could even be extended still further to include one of the new Stanier types being introduced in the interest of all-line standardization of motive power.

On reflection I chose one of the two original Midland compounds built at Derby in 1902 under the direction of S W Johnson, the Locomotive Superintendent at that time. These two beautiful engines were designed especially for working between Leeds and Carlisle. They were stationed one at each end, and for some considerable time each engine was worked by only one driver and fireman. They were magnificently finished, and because the Midland Railway had not then introduced water troughs they each had one of the huge bogie tenders. The speed on crossing Denthead Viaduct going south would be anything between 60 and 70 m.p.h. The train was running on the more or less level stretch between Hawes Junction and the start of the long descent down the Long Drag, where these two original Midland compound locomotives sometimes exceeded 90 m.p.h. I hope my picture indicates something of the speed run thereabouts.

Chapter 20
Shaldon – Teign Estuary

For some years after the dramatic episode of the wasp sting on that memorable Sunday morning, we made the family holiday at Teignmouth each summer and enjoyed the unfailing service and attention of the Bella Vista boarding house where we stayed every time. This hotel was also appreciated by some fellow guests who we met each year. They seemed to synchronize their visits for the same fortnight as ourselves and we formed a lasting, enduring and affectionate friendship. How lasting can be appreciated from my receiving in the very week I had begun to write this chapter an amusing letter from Derek Phelps, the paterfamilias, recalling that we first met 42 years ago! The friendship has continued unabated since then, although my own disability, that has precluded me from driving a car for the last eight years, has limited our contact to phone calls, the ever-welcome letters and periodic consignments of Cornish cream! They lived at Weybridge, Surrey, when we first met them, and they, like us at the start of our friendship, had to rely on travel by train. They now live in a charming country cottage near Falmouth, hence the ready supplies of Cornish cream.

Jacqueline Phelps and our Trevor, almost the same age, were passing away from the bucket and spade era and were proving delightful companions in every kind of seaside activity imaginable. They bathed, we took them for motor boat trips around the bay, and there were ever new haunts to be tried out for morning elevenses. In the meantime I myself was looking out for new subjects for water-colours. I had brought a new cheap, paint-box with me, and plenty of sketch-blocks, but the days passed so quickly with plenty of family activities that a week went by with no painting. In the meantime calm seas enticed the 'trips in the bay' motor boats to venture along the coast to give a sight of Dawlish and I was fascinated by the site of the famous red cliffs from the sea. When walking the sea wall beneath them it is strange that one cannot appreciate their texture, as it were; I am afraid my interest was more in the passing trains than in the actual geology of the cliffs themselves. Out on the sea, apart from restraining young Trevor from going overboard (!), one could study that magnificent range at leisure. I had not any colour in my camera at that time, and any photographs of the coast would have looked flat and featureless.

A thought that has come to me very many years afterwards is why did I not take the opportunity of photographing some of the trains broadside-on, from the sea. A difficulty would have occurred with timing, because the boat owners who organized 'trips in the bay' would not likely have been so railway minded as to organize excursions to synchronize with the passage of the 'Cornish Riviera Express' or the 'Torbay Limited' along the sea wall. Even so, with a little pecuniary persuasion one of them might have been induced to make a special trip for a photographic occasion – the juvenile passengers carried – and to wait abreast of the sea wall midway between Sprey Point and the Parson and Clerk rock. To make the most of the situation the day would have to be a Saturday in High Summer, when the Cornish Riviera Express was carrying its maximum load and running normally non-stop from London to Truro, with fourteen or fifteen coaches on. It would have made a great sight, photographed broadside on from the sea!

Beyond the headland tapering down to the Parson and Clerk rocks, which I had painted in the sketch so summarily interrupted on that Sunday morning, there is a short section of the railway that I had never previously seen from the outside as it were. Despite incessant vigilance, and the establishment of a 'cliff-gang' to deal with the maintenance work between Dawlish and Teignmouth, slipping gave the civil engineers continual anxiety, and in the years before the First World War a decision was taken to increase the length of the Parsons Tunnel, at the Dawlish end. The cliffs are very high above the railway hereabouts, and there had been a disastrous rock fall in broad-gauge days. The extension to the tunnel was not completed until 1921. There are some fascinating photographs of the work under construction in the little paperback, previously referred to, but the finished job is beyond public gaze, except from the sea. With the majestic background of the huge red cliffs, and the usual blue of the sea, the plain brick arch of the tunnel extension does not look very appropriate to the beautiful surroundings. I am sure that if the great Brunel had had to make that extension of the tunnel he would have done it more artistically.

From the pleasure of a gently riding motor-boat I looked across at the stretch of line between the eastern end of the Parsons Tunnel and the approach to Dawlish. The Teignmouth trips did not go as far as Dawlish itself, but I could see clearly the section where I had my tunnel adventure in 1925. The Coryton beach was usually crowded with people. Evidently they had come by boat from Dawlish because there is no footpath access. I can hardly think that any of them made their way to that beach, as I had done in 1925, through the railway tunnels! Train photographers were evidently not to be denied however, because there is one picture reproduced in that paperback of 1990 *Rails along the Sea Wall* taken in early narrow-gauge days before the line was made double-track. It shows an early Great Western 4-4-0 emerging from the single-tracked Coryton Tunnel, with the handsome entrance designed by Brunel for each of the original tunnels, of which is an impressive example, that of the west end of the Parsons Tunnel, is also illustrated in the paperback. On my own visit in 1925 I took no photographs of trains between the Coryton and Kennaway Tunnels. From the sea the cliffs were not so picturesque as when seen close at hand from the Teignmouth sea wall.

So far, it would seem, my artistic inclinations in the Teignmouth district had been concentrated on the sea wall and its sights. Far from it however. In company with the Phelps family we patronized the ferry boat across to the opposite shores of the Teign estuary, to Shaldon, and there we always found delights for our cameras, and tastes for our palettes. Shaldon and its surrounding was a charming village suburb of Teignmouth itself. I found the houses round the village green highly photogenic, and we had all walked up the stiff climb to the Ness where we were thrilled by the glorious views along the coast and also up the estuary of the River Teign. The Ness, we saw, was only the concluding feature of a long line of high cliffs that extended south-wards along the coast to the promontory known as Hope's Nose, at the northern end of Torbay. Talking of bays however, the Ordnance Survey people, on my edition of the One-Inch map, have labelled the sea bordering the cliffs from Teignmouth Ness to Hope's Nose 'Babbacombe Bay'. Anything less like a bay I find it hard to imagine, along a coast where cliffs are almost in a straight line for several miles. We walked some way along this high-elevated viewpoint, and I noted, but not at this time visited, the village of Stoke-in-Teignhead, about half a mile inland from the cliffs.

I remembered the name vividly from an excursion I made on one of my previous visits to South Devon in the mid-1920s. I cannot recall how I came to make this trip, but I remember being a somewhat unwilling participant, on a charabanc ride. I don't think the rest of the family were involved. I was persuaded to go, so I believe, because the other visitor had not a bicycle – hence the chara! Road transport by public vehicles was rather spartan in those days and the only 'guide' on the trip was the coach driver, who shouted back details of points of interest on the way. Our route from Paignton led through Torquay and then over the main road near to the cliffs towards Teignmouth, until reaching Maidencombe, where we turned off to a side road of which our charabanc scraped the hedges on both sides. Still the hot pace continued, and then the driver bawled out 'we are just coming to a pretty village, Stoke-in-Teignhead'. We roared through in a cloud of dust (!) and made our way through Combe-in-Teignhead to the banks of the Teign itself at Combe Cellars. The pub on the quayside was evidently the prime object of the trip, because nearly all the passengers, including the driver, entered in, and duly imbibed. I was barely out of my teens at the time, and very much a teetotaller. While the charabanc waited I enjoyed the river prospect and the sight of an eastbound Great Western express get-ting into its stride from Newton Abbot. There was a signal box almost opposite to Combe Cellars that I afterwards learned was named Bishopsteignton, after the nearby village. It was about half way be-tween Teignmouth and the entrance to the Newton Abbot yards, which were marked by a further signal box named Hackney.

In all my many journeys along the Great Western main line I cannot recall ever having been checked, let alone stopped at Bishopsteignton signalbox, and I have often looked across wistfully at Combe Cellars, and wished for a more extended visit than I made in the 1920s, and no doubt with some suitable refreshment. On several of my fairly recent visits to Teignmouth I have had occasional idle thoughts of Derek Phelps and I, rowing the family up the river from Shaldon, perhaps for a picnic near the Inn. But on consulting my One-Inch Ordnance Survey map I had noted that the river, while having a seemingly wide estuary, downstream from Newton Abbot has several narrow ways by which the river flows to the sea, and while at high tide the estuary was a continuous expanse of water an inexperienced navigator, such as Derek and I would undoubtedly have been, could find himself high and dry on a sandback in mid-stream as it was. On mature consideration, for an outing to Combe Cellars it seemed advisable to walk from Shaldon. After all, it was less than three miles along a country road that was never far from the shore.

I found the Teign estuary doubly delightful in the distant views it gave of the country behind Newton Abbot, with the heights of Dartmoor mounting to form an impressive and alluring background. The Hay Tor rocks from some twelve miles away can look grandly impressive but I must admit that in my earlier visits to South Devon, when my father and mother were staying in Paignton and we had a hired car and chauffeur, I directed our itineraries to less accessible but more exotic parts of the Moor, not always to the liking of our drivers! The distant prospects of Dartmoor from Shaldon, and eventually from Combe Cellars, had given me some ideas for water colours; but on this particular holiday the weather was not really suitable for sitting out and painting. I had to make rough sketches of what I proposed indoors and keep my ideas for another year. I found the immediate prospect from the beach at Shaldon just below the Ness, to give some attractive pictures so I parcelled my sketch blocks away and kept them for another year.

Next time the conditions proved to be more or less ideal. The Phelps family joined us as usual, and the young people – one must not refer to them as 'children' any longer (!) – had their own preoccupations for most of the time, and Dad could camp out and

The Teign Estuary from a deck-chair on the beach at Shaldon, looking towards Newton Abbot.

— O. S. NOCK —

paint more or less at his leisure. I cannot remember if the picture which now hangs on one of my walls, and is reproduced herewith, was done at a single session. It was painted on the beach at Shaldon, just below the Ness, but whether done at one session or more it bears unmistakeable signs of being done in a hurry. When I look back at some of my earlier drawings such as the Christmas Card of 1921, and the cottages in Clovelly High Street, and note the meticulous detail in which the structure of the cottages are portrayed, and compare them with the almost slovenly way in which those on the left-hand side bordering Shaldon village are rendered suggests that time was not on my side that particular day! On the other hand the main road-bridge spanning the estuary is accurately shown, and there was evidently time for the inclusion of the smoke of a steam train heading for Newton Abbot. On the nearer shore I painted a flotilla of rowing boats moored ready for hire, but left high and dry by the receding tide, and there was a sailing boat being navigated seaways in one of the deep water channels approaching the Shaldon beach.

I am only sorry that my viewpoint did not give a more comprehensive vista up the Teign valley and include the heights of Dartmoor. A less meticulous draughtsman than I might have rearranged the foreground a little, to give a more distant view over those cottages on the Shaldon fore-shore. But I had to be content with the fine hill, though not visible from my viewpoint, and the little village of Bishopsteignton, which gave its name to the intermediate signalbox on the Great Western main line. The Ordnance Survey map pinpoints, in Old English lettering, two features, about one quarter of a mile further inland from the village itself, as 'Bishop's Palace' and the 'Chapel'. I never found time to explore the district of Bishopsteignton so I cannot say what the relics were that were marked on the map. About three miles further west on the main road from Bishopsteignton is the larger village of Kingsteignton and as this is at the junction of the main road from Newton Abbot to Exeter I have been through it many times in my motoring days. Regarding its earlier history, and that equally of Bishopsteignton, I have recently looked up Lady Rosalind Northcote's beautiful book and she has, as might be expected, some interesting points about them both. They both mark the sites of lordly parklands of long ago, 'ancient demesnes', as Lady Northcote puts it, of the Crown, as Kingsteignton suggests, and of the See of Exeter, with Bishopsteignton. She tells a story of the latter village that the women there used to be very small, and folks said that was because they had been changed by the pixies when they were babies! Be that as it may but a Devon girl who comes from these parts, and who I know intimately, stands nearly six feet high in her stockinged feet.

Chapter 21
Wall Paintings – Railway Background

When my dear Olivia suggested that I should move Trevor's clockwork train layout from the rather gloomy kitchen annexe of our big house on Sion Hill to one of the third-floor rooms which were not being used I was delighted, because I had already added a fine Hornby 'O' gauge LNER 4-4-0 to the family rolling stock. When a second-hand Bassett Lowke *Flying Scotsman* was added to the collection, our tin-plate track although adequate did not make the best showing on the floor of that upper bedroom. Olivia again suggested that we should move the layout to one of the front bedrooms on the top floor and put the track up on permanent trestles. Before that however I had to get some more suitable track with larger radius for the curves. One could not buy anything ready-made at that time and so I had to pit my skills as a track layer building up the Bassett-Lowke coarse-scale permanent way. I found it quite rewarding as a part-time hobby – when I was not writing books, or gardening. Trevor was then away as a boarder at Monkton Combe Junior School, and the race was on to have the new track-layout and the new permanent way completed by the time he came home for the Christmas holidays.

Then Edward Beal, the authority on Model Railway construction, sent me an autographed copy of his new book *Modelling the Old-time Railways*. I was fascinated and immediately began to scheme out how the Railway Room on the top floor of No. 20 Sion Hill could be developed into a real scenic railway. We had plenty of wire netting, to provide the underlying foundation for the cardboard which was to be painted to provide the fields at the linesides, and when I went to London again I made sure of visiting the model shop near the southern end of Southampton Row where I had bought the 'O' gauge *Flying Scotsman*. There I also bought John H Ahern's lovely book *Miniature Landscape Modelling*, with an illustration on the very dust jacket that set my brain whirling with ideas for our newly established 'railway room'. This is not a book about my adventures in railway modelling, or I could gossip for pages upon pages, as to how Olivia and I schemed and contrived to produce the right effects. Yes, she was in it 'up to her ears' once Ahern's book had been thoroughly studied and digested. At first there was plenty of blank wall above the three-dimensioned portion that linked up with the track on the trestles, and as the walls had been painted in a light cream there was at first no difficulty in applying the commercial powder paint to the tints I wanted.

At Sion Hill the third-floor bedroom which we converted to the railway room was in the original part of the house and had two windows looking out and over the garden and giving a glorious view over the city and the hills on the southern side of the Avon Valley. There was a considerable space between the two windows, and the intervening wall was left blank at first. My scenic attentions were directed elsewhere. Painting on the walls involved no little thought and preparatory organization. I found it was necessary to plan the whole scene beforehand, because once the three-dimensional framework was erected one could not get to the plain walls behind for any painting. Two walls were at first concerned, and I was intrigued as to how I should treat the corner. At one time I had thought of building the join up with plaster. After all we owned the house, and within reasonable limits we could do what we liked. This was very much the case when we planned extensions from the original circuit, and starting boring holes to take branch lines through the walls into the next unoccupied bedroom. This was quite a job in itself, because the wall in question happened to be the end-wall of the original house and built as it was, virtually to stand a siege(!), it took some boring through.

However, to get back to wall painting, I had always found I could do landscapes of North-Country scenery better than I did more pastoral scenes of which there were plenty in the lush countryside in which we then lived, and I roughed out the scene that I contemplated carrying the land from the railway up to the walls in slopes that varied from pure moorland to North-Country agriculture. Olivia suggested that a farmstead should be included, and added that she would make the buildings when the time came for my provisional sketches to become three-dimensional. I carried the landscape a little up the plain wall in certain areas, and as for the sky background I added an assortment of cirrus clouds to provide a gay atmosphere to the layout generally. So the three-dimensional scenery from the track to the walls was gradually filled in.

In the space in that upper bedroom there was no room for curves of more than four-feet in radius, having provided an operating space alongside. The motive power had necessarily to be clockwork seeing that with my current pre-occupations it would often be weeks, or even months between any of the locomotives turning a wheel. Electric traction was not to be thought of, because the infrequency of usage would provide dust on the rails, and faulty contact. To disguise the relative sharpness of the curves on the end of the circuit opposite to the windows, I built a short tunnel over which I carried the bridle-path road to the farmstead buildings Olivia had built. I got out various reference books to seek out photographs of attractive tunnel façades. There was no question of trying to build a magnificent entrance like Box, which is only a few miles from where I live now. But there were many attractive ones in the books I studied, and so I got my wood-working tools together, cut the shape of the profile, and painted it up. Then there had to be a short cutting leading up to the entrance. So far so good.

That part of the line, and of course the wall painting behind, had been finished when it was time for us to go on our family holiday to the seaside. I believe it was still to Teignmouth. We left keys with certain neighbours in case of any untoward visits; but we did not reckon with the elements. During the fortnight we were away some severe storms hit the Bath area. Our neighbours went in to see that all was well, and found that some of the tiles had come loose and water had got on the walls of the railway room. They rendered first aid by putting sheets over the portion of the railway that was

affected. They also got the builder in to deal with the dislodged tiles.
But when we got home I could see there was little than could be
done about the water-stains on the wall above the farmstead, and the
landscape above the tunnel. There appeared to be nothing for it but
to rip the whole corner out and start again. At that time I had not
time to do this, so I patched it up as best I could, and when visitors
came I told the story of our storm damage.

The next piece of wall painting was between the two windows on
the outside wall. Although the curve from the passenger station was
just as sharp as that at the opposite end of the room there was no
question of disguising it this time because I had laid in some carriage
sidings parallel to the wall. As a change from the moorland country
opposite I painted an estuarine vista, with distant hills overlooking
the water-way and of course a lighthouse on the foreshore. Some of
my more enthusiastic friends though I ought to have a light bulb in
the tower and light it up at night. I must not gossip further about the
long-demolished Sion Hill railway except to include a plan of the
layout as eventually developed, because in the final extension there
were items that I have still got, and are in the picture reproduced
herewith.

Moving house to High Bannerdown, Batheaston in 1963 meant a
complete change. There was certainly no space in our new house for
anything approaching a model railway, but there was plenty of space
in our new large garden, and so I got my drawing instruments together, and schemed out the design of a 'Railway House' which
could conveniently be built in the garden. It was to be no half-
hearted affair, no mere shack, but a solidly built house of brick and
stone to match in with the attractive particular style of our newly
acquired dwelling house. The Railway House was to be at least 50 ft.
long and 25 ft. wide. It would be heated, have a handsome garden
frontage, and include space for a small workshop and an entrance
area where I could mount the growing collection of railway coats of
arms we were acquiring. The additional space gave the opportunity
to lay in curves of considerably larger radius than had been possible
at Sion Hill, and this greatly improved the running. Painting the
walls gave me tremendous scope. The rooms would be newly deco-
rated and I could get the builders to paint the background walls to

Wall painting behind the railway layout in the library at 28 High Bannerdown.

where the railway would be with a limpid sky-blue colour on which I could add such cloud effects as I fancied. On the Silver Cedars Railway House nearly all the scenery was three-dimensional and it was only the background to the running shed on which I had occasion to apply my brushes. Here I continued the idea I had begun at Sion Hill by putting a semi-industrial background to the round-house, which I had modelled on that of Inverness.

Before leaving Sion Hill I had obtained detailed drawings of what the original roundhouse of the Inverness and Aberdeen Junction Railway was like, and this was eventually enlarged to make an almost complete circle, leaving only the ornate ornamental water-tower spanning the entrance tracks. Then I made the timber framework of the shed, and mounted it on an appropriate base-board, and that was as far as the roundhouse progressed at Sion Hill. It could readily be transported to the new site in High Bannerdown, and there I continued putting the roof on and the encircling walls. But there was so much more to do on the big layout that I was building at Silver Cedars to say nothing of running some trains (!), that the completion of the roundhouse structure was awarded a relatively low priority. Once arrived in High Bannerdown we found we had some very friendly neighbours. Without being at any way 'nosy' they became interested in the building of the 'Railway House', and when the first circuit of track was laid, but before any wall painting was done, we had a little party and ran some trains. Although we lived at Silver Cedars for seventeen years such was the extent of my other preoccupations, including a number of tours far overseas to collect data for book writing, that the scenic background for this large railway was never entirely completed, one notable omission being the completion of the roundhouse.

Then there came the time when Olivia and I decided that we did not need such a big establishment. Our family were away from home and settled down, and while a move to smaller quarters would inevitably mean giving up The Railway House and all that was contained therein we both felt it was time to relax a little. There was a vacant plot of land higher up the road in High Bannerdown. We found the owner was one of the neighbours who had been very friendly to us, and after preliminary exchanges I sketched out the plan of the much reduced-size dwelling we felt we needed. The owner of the plot was one of the leading architects in Bath, and his office quickly transformed my sketches into a beautiful plan which was duly submitted to the authority for planning permission. The new layout included a library of a size that permitted a small layout of railway tracks and the Inverness roundhouse. There would be no space to do any actual running, and most of my coaching stock would have to be disposed of. I kept one coach out of each train as a souvenir of old times, and with the coaches went the commercially-made locomotives, the Bassett-Lowke *Flying Scotsman,* and the *King George V,* and several Hornby 4-4-0s.

A space no more than 8 ft. square was all that could be given up to the new layout, but into this I contrived to pack my model of the Inverness roundhouse, the appropriate approach tracks and some engine sidings, and the coaling stage, and of course the ornamental water tower. I had thirteen locomotives left, all but one clockwork, and the carriage stock remaining consisted of LNWR composite corridor latest type, GWR clerestory-roofed corridor, GWR 70-foot corridor coach, GNR 12-wheeled dining car, GNR pre-corridor 6-wheeled main line coach, Highland 1915 vintage TPO bogie sorting van with traductor apparatus, LNWR 6-wheeled parcel-post sorting van, LNWR small 4-wheeled carriage. Because of the limited space there was no room for any three-dimensional work between the buildings and the walls and the scene painting on the walls had to blend in with the roundhouse. The limited space in our new house meant all the railway equipment had to be parked elsewhere while the background scene was being painted. Fortunately I had stipulated with the carpenters who were building the 8 ft. square erection that was to carry the roundhouse layout that the boards of the staging were to be made loose so that I could remove them when engaged on wall painting. As at Silver Cedars I had the sky painted ready for me to add the cloud effects.

The immediate background gave me some concern. Of course there was the case for repeating the treatment I had given on the walls of the third room at Sion Hill where the skeleton of the roundhouse had first been installed. There I had painted an industrial background hoping it would look like Inverness itself with the towers of the cathedral in the distance. In my new layout I felt that some attention should be given to the wide variety to say nothing of the dates of construction of the locomotives. I had nothing but express passenger types dating between 1880 and 1935, and on railways ranging from the Great Western, London and North Western, Midland, Great Northern, North Eastern, Furness, Caledonian, North British and Highland. There were also two from the post-grouping era, one LMS and one LNER. How could a scenic background reflect on the previous association of such a variety? There had also to be some indication of the means of access to the shed. I felt that one could not dump a relatively large roundhouse on a baseboard without giving something of the way it was approached. The coaling stage also gave me some food for thought.

This last feature proved the determining factor in the whole scheme of wall decoration. The roundhouse had essentially to be in the right-hand corner which made it necessary for the approach tracks and coaling stage connection to be on the left. In the Silver Cedars layout I had built an arched approach to the coaling stage spanning tracks that were the culminating point of a series of carriage sidings. In the new layout, with most of carriage stock disposed of, the arches, which I had retained, seemed to have no useful purpose, until I conceived the idea of having short sidings under the arches to which access was made from single-wagon turntables on the locomotive roads from the coaling plant. The track beyond the arches was blended into the background under which the main access line form the shed was carried through a short 'tunnel' at right angles to the wall of the room, with the view through it painted on the wall. No more than the outskirts of the town where the locomotive men and the shed staff lived is shown on the extreme left-hand end of the wall painting. The main-wall picture shows upland country typical, I hope, of the eastern side of the Scottish Highlands, with the hills not rising more than about 2000 ft., with the lower slopes cultivated, and a golf course beside the main line of the railway. This line soon enters a tunnel in the hillside, from which, further up, two successive ventilating shafts can be seen smoking. On the right of the scene is the estuary of a river, which on the eastern seabord of Scotland would be known as a 'firth', as distinct from the sea-lochs in the Western Highlands. The roundhouse was situated on higher ground above the shores of the 'firth'.

Chapter 22
'The Silver Jubilee'

As far as I can trace, the first public announcement of a new, high-speed express train service between Kings Cross and Newcastle came early in April 1935. It came as a result of the very successful and at times spectacular results of the trial runs on 5 March when the feasibility of a 4-hour timing between London and Newcastle was convincingly demonstrated with an ordinary Gresley 'Pacific' engine and standard rolling stock. It was stated that although the runs of 5 March had shown that nothing new was needed it was felt that the construction of a new fully streamlined train was desirable to provide the publicity for this very special year of celebrations, and because of the time needed to design and build the new train and locomotives the new service would not begin operation until 30 September. *The Railway Gazette* of 16 August included the note that already a large number of reservations of seats for the inaugural run on 30 September had been made. The latest of these reservations came from as far abroad as Australia and India and there were indications that a number of Americans on holiday in this country were intending to travel on the new train before returning to the USA.

Just over a month later *The Railway Gazette* carried a magnificently illustrated article describing the new train in full detail. I saw the first streamlined engine the *Silver Link* soon afterwards and I must confess that I was not very impressed. But my dear wife who in her spinster days was on the staff of the Hotels and Restaurant Car Department of the LNER and then stationed at Kings Cross, was thrilled beyond measure. My own slight cynicism was considerably tempered when I read of the well-nigh sensational speed achieve-

ments on the demonstration run of 27 September. The general
public, still less the technical press, were not told the reasons for the
tremendous spell of high speed put on between Potters Bar and the
approach to Offord on that memorable afternoon. In the article
published in *The Railway Gazette* a week earlier the schedules planned
for the new train were published, giving the passing times at the
principal stations and junctions. On the southbound run the average
speeds were quoted as 77.0 m.p.h. from Eryholme Junction to
Northallerton, thence to Thirsk, 77.5 m.p.h., and on to Alne, 82.7
m.p.h. With a superb track and an almost level road such speeds
were often sustained with far heavier trains than the 220-ton 'Silver
Jubilee' with standard non-streamlined corridor stock, and ordinary
'Pacific' engines. That this was well known to the compilers of the
logs of train running speeds as quoted in the British 'Locomotive
Practice and Performance' feature in *The Railway Magazine* was not
so well known to many technical staff of the engineering departments of the LNER.

By the beginning of the year 1934 the resignalling of the East
Coast main line between York and Northallerton had been completed, using, principally, three-indication searchlight signals spaced
about 1330 yards apart on a plain line. This spacing was apparently
adequate to provide ample braking distance for express passenger
trains running at a speed of 70 m.p.h. The fastest existing run was
timed at a little under 62 m.p.h. start-to-stop between Darlington
and York, but that this train frequently exceeded a speed of 80
m.p.h. was not generally known to the engineering departments.
Then, when the speeds programmed for 'The Silver Jubilee' were
published in *The Railway Gazette* there was consternation in some
quarters because the new colourlight signalling between York and
Northallerton did not allow sufficient braking distance for the
speeds that were scheduled. With such an average speed as 82.7
m.p.h. from Thirsk to Alne, the maximum speed could well be approaching 87 to 88 m.p.h. This, the civil engineering people said,
was unsafe and could mean that signals would be overrun. At that
time I should explain that signalling came within the domain of the
Chief Engineer for each Region of the LNER. South of York the
signalling on the rest of the line to Kings Cross was still ordinary

manual block, and the progress of 'The Silver Jubilee' was safe-
guarded by a special regulation that the signalmen could not lower
their semaphore signals to give 'line clear' to the train unless two
block sections ahead were clear.

In view of this restriction the working times over the 44.1 miles
between York and Darlington were amended thus: southbound from
37 minutes to 41 minutes, and northbound from 39 minutes to $41\frac{1}{2}$
minutes. Small adjustments to the timings south of York were made
to maintain the advertised overall of 4 hours between Kings Cross
and Newcastle. The demonstration run on 27 September was made
not only for the edification of the Press but to see what margin was in
reserve in the modified schedule after adjustments had been made
to the timings north of York. Between Kings Cross and Peterborough, the section over which the record-breaking speeds were run
on 27 September, the differences in the published schedule quoted
in the article in *The Railway Gazette* of 20 September and those actually put into operation on 30 September were:

Kings Cross	depart min	0	0
Hatfield	pass	18	$18\frac{1}{2}$
Hitchin	pass	29	$29\frac{1}{2}$
Huntingdon	pass	49	$48\frac{1}{2}$
Peterborough	pass	65	$63\frac{1}{2}$

Well, margin in reserve? – the demonstration train on 27 September
went through Peterborough in just two seconds over 55 minutes!
The Locomotive Running Superintendent of the Southern Area of
the LNER himself rode on the footplate of the engine *Silver Link*, as
if to 'see fair play' as it were, and while the speed rose to a peak of
$112\frac{1}{2}$ m.p.h. twice the engine and tender gave him an immaculately
smooth ride and he had no occasion to impose any restraint on the
driver.

In the train however it was not so comfortable. Gresley nevertheless was imperturable and armed with a huge stop-watch was enjoying
every minute of it, never more so when he was chaffing the Chief
Civil Engineer about a stretch of apparently rough track that they
had then encountered. But after passing St Neots, at over 100 m.p.h.,

and with the speed again rising, the reverse curves on the banks of the River Ouse were just ahead; and while with excellent track and first class rolling stock going round those curves could be quite comfortable at 80 m.p.h., at 100 m.p.h. it could well have been another matter, and Gresley himself went through the corridor tender on to the footplate and advised the driver to ease up a little. Actually the speed was reduced from 109½ m.p.h. to 85 m.p.h. round the curves. For regular service on 'The Silver Jubilee' the streamlined 'Pacific' engines were fitted with the Flaman speed recorder in their cabs whereby a graphic record of the speeds maintained throughout the run were registered. At the end of the journey the charts were removed from the instrument and taken at once to the Running Superintendent's office for an independent examination. At the beginning of the new service a specially chosen quartet of drivers from the No. 1 link at Kings Cross top shed were the only ones allowed to work 'The Silver Jubilee'. Of the four new streamlined 'Pacific' locomotives, classed as 'A4', three of them, *Silver Link, Quicksilver* and *Silver Fox,* were stationed at Kings Cross. The London men worked the down train, lodged the night, and brought the train south next morning. The fourth engine, the *Silver King,* was stationed at Gateshead as a reserve in Newcastle in case any temporary defect kept the booked engine from going south.

Gresley allowed a reproduction of one of the speed charts from the Flaman recorder to be published in *The Railway Magazine* of August 1936. I fancy Charles Doncaster's photograph, which I painted some years afterwards, must have been taken at much the same time. On the chart the graph of the speed shows a severe slowing down south of Doncaster for permanent way work, and recovery to normal speed in that area had not taken place by the time the train had passed Bawtry. The photograph shows clearly that the engine was being steamed hard as if to recover the normal speed. The smoke effect is most satisfying. Doncaster told me he was lucky not to be drenched to the skin in a heavy thunderstorm that swept over the area soon afterwards. The sky background in his photograph, which I have tried to reproduce in my painting, clearly indicates some stormy weather coming in from the east. In ordinary service on this high-speed train the maximum speed was generally agreed to be about 90

'The Silver Jubilee', southbound, at high speed near Bawtry in 1937.

m.p.h. This was sufficient to provide a recovery margin for all the incident slowings, for temporary track repairs and so on. On the chart published in *The Railway Magazine* there were four engineering slacks, in addition to the regular speed restrictions through the stations at York, Selby and Peterborough. On the famous racing stretch from Stoke tunnel down towards Peterborough the speed was maintained steadily at around 90 m.p.h.

It was far otherwise on 27 August 1936. The success of 'The Silver Jubilee' train was leading the top management of the LNER to thoughts of extending the streamlined train service to Edinburgh in 1937, which would be the Coronation Year of King George VI, and Queen Elizabeth, and on that August day arrangements had been made to attach the former NER dynamometer car to the Silver Jubilee on its regular runs and so to obtain a continuous record of the drawbar pull and other technical data of the performance. This put the tare weight of the train up to 254 tons. On the southbound journey the engine was the *Silver Fox*, driven by George Haygreen, one of the elite quartet, and one of the most expert and accurate drivers I have ever personally known. One of his regular fireman once said of him: 'Time keeping, he could split a second!' I came to know him well quite apart from railways. One of his daughters was on my staff at Westinghouse as a junior typist. On 27 August, apart from having a technical observer on the footplate as well as a locomotive inspector, things went normally as far south as Grantham, and then a very senior officer of the Chief Mechanical Engineer's department came through the corridor tender and positioned himself behind the driver.

After passing Stoke summit Haygreen began to adjust his controls to make a normal descent towards Peterborough when this engineer, who should have known better, said 'Top a hundred!' They had passed Corby by then and were doing no more than 85 m.p.h. But instructions were instructions and Haygreen began opening out, and so vigorously did he do so that the speed had increased to more than 105 m.p.h at Little Bytham. Some relaxation was needed then, but this high official demanded more, and the hapless driver had to open out still further before Essendine. It was not until they were nearing Tallington that this imperious individual decided to leave the footplate, and by that time the speed had reached 113 m.p.h. This was not only 0.5 m.p.h. faster than the record twice attained by *Silver Link* on 27 September 1935, but in surpassing their previous record it marked by far the highest speed attained by a British train conveying ordinary fare-paying passengers. It is true that the dynamometer car was in use, taking many technical details of the performance but behind the car was a full load of passengers. On 27 September the train was certainly fairly full, but the passengers were all invited guests of the LNER, many of them representatives of the daily and technical press. Driver Haygreen himself was not proud of his achievements that day. In any case the sudden demand for an exceptional effort led to the engine developing heating troubles and not being able to make the return run with the dynamometer car that same evening. On arrival at Kings Cross shed, the special test fittings had to be removed and transferred to *Silver Link*, which was prepared for any such emergency. Haygreen talking to me privately some time afterwards said that if only they had let him know what they wanted previously he would have gone up the bank from Grantham much harder. They had plenty of steam, and the speed at Stoke summit could easily have been 75 m.p.h., instead of a little over 60. That would have given them a better start to a really fast descent of the bank towards Peterborough and the speed could have been 95 m.p.h. when passing Corby instead of the 85 m.p.h. it actually was. Nevertheless George Haygreen remains the driver who attained the highest speed on British railways with a steam-hauled train conveying a full load of ordinary fare-paying passengers.

Some three weeks later I had occasion to travel north by 'The Silver Jubilee' on the first stage of a late fortnight's holiday in Scotland. Violet Haygreen knew about this and a few days before I went she told me that her father would be driving the train that night and would I like to go through to the footplate at some part of the journey. It was a very tempting invitation. The door to the corridor tender was nearly always unlocked and I could make a discreet entry at some time. But no! I knew from other sources how complete an embargo on footplate passes for 'The Silver Jubilee' had been imposed by high authority, and if I was caught not only would it get the driver into trouble but it would undoubtedly put a full stop to the many other footplate passes I had enjoyed from the LNER, and to the others I looked forward to in the future. Even so when I walked up the platform to see the engine before we started on this particular journey the fireman of the *Silver Link* met me with a broad smile: 'Are you coming through?' he asked. He it was who averred that George Haygreen was such an accurate timekeeper that he could split a second. The temptation was renewed, and in the presence of the travelling ticket collector who would be riding on the train. But the risks, I felt, were too great.

The journey itself proceeded normally. Knowing there was going to be a slight engineering delay near Doncaster, Haygreen had got a minute or so in hand on passing Retford, 138½ miles from Kings Cross, in 112 minutes. But the delay was worse than he expected, and we were nearly four minutes late in passing slowly through the great station at York, although it was a calm fine evening in late summer. On the fine straight level track across the plain of York the searchlight colour light signals stood out with amazing clarity, and with the 70 m.p.h. speed limit now observed more in the spirit than in the letter the driver went for it. Before the first station north of York the speed was 82 m.p.h. We reached a level 90 m.p.h. after Alne, and Thirsk was passed on time. On arrival at Darlington we were nearly three minutes early. Before leaving the station I went up to the engine again to be greeted again by that enthusiastic fireman: 'What do you think of that, for a bit of stuff?'

The four streamlined 'Pacifics' built specially for 'The Silver Jubilee' service were the only ones ever painted in the striking silver livery. When more of the 'A4' class were built, in anticipation of further high-speed trains, in Coronation Year, the intention was at first to finish them in the standard green livery used for the older 'Pacifics' and other top-line express passenger engines. The first new one built at Doncaster, the *Golden Eagle*, and several more were painted green, and then, with the introduction of the new streamlined 'Coronation', the engines were to be painted 'Garter Blue' in honour of the Royal event. So that by mid-summer 1937 the LNER had streamlined 'Pacific' engines in silver, green and blue! At first some attempt was made to couple the silver engines to the 'Jubilee' and the blue engines to the 'Coronation', but this was proved impracticable eventually and so early in 1938 the decision was taken that all the 'A4' class engines should be painted Garter Blue. When three times I travelled by 'The Silver Jubilee' in the early spring of 1939 the engines successively were *Silver Link, Silver Fox,* and *Dominion of New Zealand,* all in blue. The silver livery on the Jubilee engines must have been the shortest lived of any on British express locomotives. In painting Charles Doncaster's picture of *Quicksilver* in silver at speed near Bawtry I dedicated it to my dear wife, Olivia, and it hung on one of her walls for many years. It has only recently been taken down for photographing in readiness for the present book.

Index